Suretha du Toit

Happy birthday!

All about children's parties

Tafelberg

Cover design by G&G Design
Photography by Paul Swart
Illustrations by Dianne Minnaar
Set in 11 on 13 pt Times
by Diatype Setting, Cape Town
Lithographic reproduction Syreline, Cape Town
Printed and bound by National Book Printers,
Goodwood, C.P.
First edition, first impression 1985

ISBN 0 624 02186 6

Contents

Types of topping

Fluffy white icing

400 g (500 ml) sugar
250 ml water
4 egg whites
24 white marshmallows

1. Whisk egg whites well, set aside.
2. With a pair of scissors cut up the marshmallows into small pieces and set aside.
3. Boil sugar and water together until the soft ball stage is reached (122°C).
4. To determine if this stage has been reached, drop a little of the sugar mixture into a glass of cold water. If a soft ball forms, the mixture is ready.
5. Cook a further minute and pour gradually over whisked egg whites, beating mixture continuously.
6. Mix the marshmallow pieces into the icing.

Butter icing

100 g (125 ml) butter or margarine
250 g (500 ml) icing sugar
10 ml vanilla essence
a little milk

1. Cream butter or margarine with icing sugar.
2. Flavour with vanilla essence and add a little milk until a soft icing consistency is reached.

Fondant

100 ml liquid glucose (obtainable at chemists)
4 egg whites
3 packets (500 g each) icing sugar, sifted
25 ml cornflour
colouring powder

1. Heat bottle of glucose for 5 minutes in hot water, or for 30 seconds in a microwave oven.
2. Put egg whites in a bowl. Add sifted icing sugar, a little at a time, mixing it in with a knife. Finish mixing by hand until a stiff paste forms. The fondant should have the consistency of putty.
3. Knead in glucose and cornflour.
4. Knead in colouring powder.
5. Place fondant in a plastic bag and leave for at least 2 hours to make it more elastic and pliable.
6. Shape trees, animals, flowers, etc. from the fondant, or roll it out thinly and press out shapes.

Butter glacé

20 g (25 ml) butter or margarine
250 g (500 ml) icing sugar
a little milk

1. Mix shortening and icing sugar.
2. Add a little milk and mix well.

Water icing

icing sugar
water
colouring

1. Mix icing sugar with enough water to obtain a dropping consistency (adjust quantities according to need). Icing must not be too thin.
2. Colour as required.

Royal icing

1 egg white
3 drops lemon juice
175 g (330 ml) icing sugar, sifted
colouring and flavouring (optional)

1. Mix egg white and lemon juice in a bowl.
2. Add sifted icing sugar in spoonsful and mix until icing holds its shape.
3. Colour and/or flavour if desired.
4. Seal bowl tightly until needed or the icing will dry out.

Cooked frosting

450 g (560 ml) sugar
140 ml water
2 egg whites

1. Dissolve sugar in water, stirring continuously. Bring to the boil, without stirring, and boil until the soft ball stage is reached (122°C).
2. Whisk egg whites stiffly.
3. Pour syrup over whisked egg whites and beat with a wooden spoon until mixture coats back of spoon.
4. Ice the cake quickly.

Uncooked frosting

2 egg whites
3 ml cream of tartar
420 g (800 ml) icing sugar
(makes 500 ml)

1. Whisk egg whites and cream of tartar until whisk leaves a trail when lifted.
2. Add half the icing sugar and beat for 10 minutes, or until frosting forms stiff peaks. Add remaining icing sugar.
3. Beat another 5 to 10 minutes, until frosting is thick and stiff.

Hint
Frosting dries out quickly. If it is not to be used immediately, store, sealed, in the refrigerator.

Instant plastic icing

Instant plastic icing is available from any shop that specialises in cake trimmings and associated items. It is usually sold by the kilogram.

Marzipan for moulding

350 g Peter Pan marzipan
250 g (480 ml) icing sugar, sifted
10 ml gelatine
½ egg white
colouring

1. Place marzipan in a lukewarm oven for a few minutes, and heat to about 40°C.
2. Grease a mixing bowl with vegetable oil.
3. Add icing sugar to bowl and heat over boiling water.
4. Sprinkle gelatine over 10 ml cold water in a separate bowl and stir. Add 10 ml boiling water, and dissolve gelatine over boiling water.
5. Remove bowl of icing sugar from heat, make a well in the centre and add the gelatine and egg white. Stir well, then work in the warm marzipan.
6. Rub your hands with vegetable oil and knead paste well.
7. Leave to cool, then add colouring.

Hint
Store colours separately in plastic bags, in a sealed container in the refrigerator.

Homemade piping bag

When using large quantities of icing, it is convenient to use a piping bag rather than a small piping tube. Piping bags can be bought, but it is quick and easy to make one from paper:

1. Cut butter-paper (250 mm x 250 mm) diagonally to form two triangles.
2. Hold apex of the triangle between thumb and index finger. Curl the right hand corner around the fingers to form a narrow 'funnel' (see first illustration on opposite page).
3. Curl left hand corner around to the corner held by the fingers (see second illustration). The opening at the bottom should be kept small.
4. Fold corners to the inside to keep paper in place.

5. Snip off bottom of the bag just enough to fit the icing nozzle tightly. Drop icing nozzle into the bag — about one-third of its point should protrude from the opening.

6. Icing nozzles are sold by numbers, for example 8, 12, etc., and they are about 25 mm in diameter at the open end.

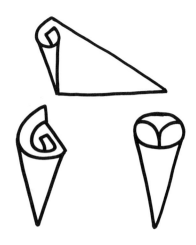

Invitations and birthday cards

Invitations

Clothes-pegs

1. Glue any picture (a butterfly or frog, etc.) onto a clothes-peg as decoration; a child can draw his own pictures, or cut them out.
2. Write an invitation on paper or a card.
3. Clasp with the clothes-peg. Give it to the guest or drop it into his letter box.

Match-boxes

1. Place an invitation inside a match-box. A sweet can be put inside with it.
2. Wrap up the box and deliver to a friend.

Colourful flags

1. Use a short stick and glue a coloured or plain piece of paper to it to look like a little flag.
2. Write an invitation on the flag, wrap it around the 'flagpole' and deliver.

Plain invitations

1. Buy printed invitation cards.
2. Let the child write his own name on the cards. Let those who cannot yet write pretend they are writing.

Balloon invitations

1. Write an invitation on a piece of paper and fold it as small as possible.
2. Place it inside a balloon. Inflate the balloon and knot or tie up the end.
3. To read the invitation, the recipient has to burst the balloon.

Clothes-pegs invitations (left), teaser invitations (right) and a sweet invitation (middle, below).

Teasers

1. Instead of giving each child a teaser at the party, an invitation can be stuck to the end of the teaser.
2. When the child blows the teaser, the invitation jumps out.

A sweet invitation

1. Use fondant or plastic icing. Roll it into a thin layer.
2. Press out shapes with fancy cutters and allow shapes to dry out completely (at least two days).
3. Write on the invitation with vegetable colouring, a pencil or a non-toxic felt-tip pen.
4. Place the sweet invitation in an envelope and deliver.

Hat

1. Make a paper hat.
2. Decorate it and write the invitation on the hat.
3. Tell the guests to wear their hats to the party.

Birthday cards

Lace decoration

1. Using a piece of coloured cardboard or stiff paper, glue a strip of lace around the edges.
2. A picture can be drawn between the borders, or a suitable message or rhyme written.

Rickrack braid

1. Coil up a piece of rickrack braid to form a flower.
2. Glue the bottom end and stick it to a card made from stiff paper or cardboard.

Balloons

1. Inflate one balloon for each year of the child's age and tie them to a birthday gift.
2. Write a congratulatory message with a felt-tip pen on each of the balloons, or number them.

11

Right: Novel birthday cards can be made out of basic material like cardboard or stiff paper, rickrack braid or bias binding and pictures that have been cut out.
Below: Decorations for birthday cards.

Left: Money and a birthday wish placed in an ordinary envelope become a colourful gift if decorated with a picture.
Below: Examples of money-cards.

A sweet birthday card

1. Cover a piece of stiff cardboard with aluminium foil.
2. Provide your child with an assortment of sweets, biscuits, etc. and a bowl of royal icing (see p. 7) for sticking the sweets to the foil. He can then design and make his own edible birthday card.

Envelope

1. Use a plain envelope and put a birthday card and some money for a present inside.
2. Decorate envelope as shown in the examples above.

Money-cards

1. Draw or cut out a picture and stick it to a piece of cardboard.
2. Stick coins to this picture, as shown.

Gift wrapping and small gifts

Gift wrapping

Let the child make his own drawings on a sheet of paper and wrap the gift with it.

A small gift can be wrapped in a nice handkerchief.

Splatter or blow paint onto the paper. Leave to dry before wrapping gift.

Small gifts

If the child is still too small to make the following gifts by himself, Mom or Dad will have to help.

Crayon container

an empty tin, open at one end
a piece of cloth, plastic or paper
strong glue
rickrack braid, lace or ribbon

1. Remove the wrapping and clean the tin with a rag.
2. Measure the circumference and height of the tin and cut the material accordingly.
3. Glue the cloth firmly to the tin.
4. Finish off by decorating with rickrack braid around the bottom and top of the tin.
5. Leave to dry properly.

The partygoer can wrap a present in his very own work of art.

14

Pin bowling.

Rattle

a tin with a screw top
little stones
paint

1. Place the stones inside the tin.
2. Use bigger stones for a louder, rougher sound; small stones will give a softer, thinner sound.
3. Screw the top on tightly.
4. Decorate the tin by painting on patterns, a face or any other picture.

Pin bowling

4 empty plastic bottles
4 colours of paint
a bean bag or ball

1. Paint each bottle a different colour.
2. The children try to bowl over the bottles from a distance with the bean bag or ball. Points are scored when different values are given to each colour.

Wooden horse

man's stretch sock
upholstery material (reject pieces of material, foam rubber or old nylons)
an old broomstick or other smooth piece of timber
glue
string or twine
reject cloth or felt
leather strips, ribbon or rope
left-over lengths of wool

1. Stuff sock with upholstery material.
2. Force the broomstick as far as possible into the sock.
3. Glue the top edge of sock to the broomstick. Tie it firmly with string.
4. Make the eyes, ears, nose, etc. with pieces of material and affix to the head (glue or sew).
5. Make the bridle and reins from leather strips, ribbon or rope and sew them on.
6. Stick or sew on pieces of wool for the mane. Paint broomstick with non-toxic enamel paint.

15

Glitter bottle

a glass or plastic bottle with top (plastic is safer!)
water
glitter (obtainable at stationers or chain stores) − blue, green, gold or silver
a small plastic toy or other suitable object

1. Fill bottle almost to the top with water.
2. Add glitter (a heaped teaspoonful) to the water. If you have various colours, they can be mixed.
3. Place toy or other object in the bottle.
4. Screw on bottle top tightly.

Parachute

a large paper plate
a large plastic bag
a sharp nail or needle
8 lengths of string or wool, 400 mm long
a yoghurt cup
small stone

1. Use paper plate as guide and cut a circle from the plastic bag.
2. Use the nail or needle to make 8 holes about 90 mm apart on the circumference of the plastic circle.
3. Push a piece of string through each hole and tie.
4. Pierce four holes through the brim of the yoghurt cup and push the eight strings through them, in pairs, then tie.
5. Ensure all strings are now of equal length. Put a small stone into the cup. If dropped from a height, the parachute will slowly float down.

Binoculars

2 empty toilet paper rolls
aluminium foil
glue
a piece of string or wool

1. Measure two equal strips of foil and cover each roll with foil and smooth down firmly.
2. Glue the two toilet paper rolls together lengthwise.
3. Pierce a hole through the outside of each roll near the end.
4. Tie a string through the holes, long enough to allow the binoculars to be hung around the neck.

Wooden dominoes

any number of wooden pieces, each 50 mm x 100 mm, made of plywood or hardboard
marking pencil
4 or 5 different colours of paint
paint brush
sanding paper

1. Mark off each of the wooden pieces into two squares, each 50 mm x 50 mm.
2. Paint each square a different colour. Vary the combinations so that the blocks do not all look alike.
3. Leave paint to dry, sand down lightly and give another coat of paint if necessary.
4. Play as with dominoes − using corresponding colours instead of numbers (dots).

Useful containers

The following reject items can be most useful for parties when converted to something novel: egg trays, toilet paper rolls, paper plates, margarine containers and bags.

Animals, insects and flowers can be made from empty egg trays.

Egg trays

Bees

empty egg tray
sweets
glue and yellow paint
yellow serviette
black felt pen
1 pipe-cleaner, cut in half

1. Cut four small cups from the egg tray (see figure below).
2. Fill the cups with sweets.
3. Glue the cups together in pairs to form the bee's body.
4. Paint the 'body' yellow and leave to dry.
5. Cut wings from a yellow serviette and glue onto body.
6. Draw the face and lines on the yellow body using a thick black felt pen.
7. Make feelers with the pipe-cleaner.

Flowers

empty egg tray
paint
drinking straw
hundreds and thousands
royal icing
any round sweet

1. Cut a cup from the egg tray and make six cuts in it to form petals (see figure below).
2. Paint the flower any bright colour and leave to dry.
3. A drinking straw is used for the flower's stem and it can be filled with hundreds and thousands.
4. Glue or staple the stem to the flower.
5. Stick a flat round sweet with royal icing to the centre of the flower.

More egg tray figurines: frogs, dogs, manikins and a spider.

Empty toilet paper rolls can be used to make a train, a funny face, a house, bunny, dachshund and crackers, and lots of other figurines. Above: The forming of the dachshund's nose.

Frog

empty egg tray
sweets
glue
green paint
green paper

1. Cut two cups from the egg tray and fill them with sweets, then glue the cups together.
2. Paint this 'body' green.
3. Cut the frog's feet from green paper and glue to the body.
4. Glue on the eyes and draw the mouth with a pen.

Duckling

empty egg tray
sweets
glue
paint (yellow or orange)
orange paper

1. Cut two cups from the egg tray. Fill them with sweets and glue them together.
2. Paint the 'body' orange or yellow.
3. Cut the feet and beak from orange coloured paper and glue them to body.

A spider, doll, bear, dog, worm, etc., can be made along the same principle. The flat half of the egg tray can be used for a boat or a garden.

Toilet paper rolls

Crackers

empty toilet paper roll
crinkle paper
ribbon
decorations
confectionery

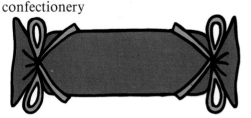

1. Wrap crinkle paper around the roll. Tie up one end with a bow and fill cracker with confectionery.
2. Tie up other end similarly and decorate cracker with pictures, glitter, brightly coloured bows, flowers, etc.

Funny faces

empty toilet paper roll
paper
paint
decorations

1. Cover open ends of the empty roll with paper.
2. Paint the roll, then draw a funny face on it.
3. Cut ears, feet and hands from paper and glue them to the body.
4. Decorate further with buttons, wool, lace, net, etc.

Train

empty toilet paper roll
confectionery
black paper or paint
small empty *Smartie* box
glue
milk bottle tops
cork
white cotton wool
square or oblong sweets

1. Fill toilet roll with confectionery and cover the roll with black paper.
2. Cover *Smartie* box with black paper and glue it to the one end of the roll.
3. Use milk bottle tops for the train wheels and cork for the smoke stack. Use glue to attach them.
4. A piece of cotton wool on the cork will look like smoke.
5. Use small square or oblong sweets for the windows.

19

Dachshund

empty toilet paper roll
confectionery, paper and glue

1. Fill the roll with confectionery and cover ends with paper.
2. Make ears and tail from paper, glue them on and leave to dry.

Above: The forming of the Dachshund's nose.

House

empty toilet paper roll
paper
glue
confectionery
paint

1. Cover one end of the roll with paper and fill with confectionery.
2. Make roof from a circular piece of paper by cutting it once from the edge to the centre and folding it to form a funnel.
3. Glue roof to the other end of the roll. Paint it and draw a window and door.

Bunny

empty toilet paper roll
paper and glue
confectionery
paint

1. Fill paper roll with confectionery and cover both open ends with paper.
2. Paint the roll and leave to dry.
3. Cut ears and feet from paper or cardboard and glue them on.
5. Make a fluffy tail from cotton wool and glue it on.

Paper plates

Faces

large or small paper plates
decorations (*Smarties*, marshmallows, chips, *Nik-Naks*, etc.)
royal icing
serviettes
black felt pen

1. Stick various types of decoration to the plates with royal icing.
2. Draw remainder of the face with a thick black felt pen. Make hats and ears from folded serviettes and stick on.

These plates give the children something to eat while at the same time serving as a 'fun' dish for other snacks. A variety of faces can be drawn, for example a cat, pig, girl, clown, clock, duckling, etc.

Paper plates decorated with snacks and serviettes not only give the children something to eat, but contribute to the party atmosphere by serving as 'fun dishes' for other snacks.

21

Margarine containers

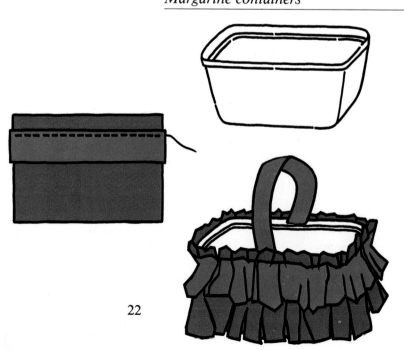

Basket

empty margarine container
crinkle paper, glue and cardboard
confectionery

1. Clean margarine container thoroughly.
2. Cut a straight strip of crinkle paper as wide as the depth of the margarine container.
3. Stitch a gathered pleat down the middle of the crinkle paper.
4. Pull the tacking or gathering thread until the strip fits round the container, then glue it on.
5. Cut a handle from cardboard and glue the ends to the opposite sides of the basket, on the inside.
6. Fill the basket with confectionery.

22

Bunny

empty margarine container
cardboard
glue
royal icing
marshmallow
confectionery

1. Clean margarine container thoroughly.
2. Cut two large ears from cardboard and glue them to the front of the container.
3. Use royal icing to stick a white marshmallow to the other end.
4. Draw bunny's face on cardboard and cut it out, then glue it to the face end of the container below the ears.
5. Fill container with confectionery.

Duckling

empty margarine container
yellow crinkle paper
orange paper

1. Cover the margarine container with yellow crinkle paper. Cut a face, tail and wings from orange paper (see photograph on p. 22), then glue them to the body.
2. Fill the container with sweets.

Car

empty margarine container
aluminium foil
royal icing
round biscuits
edible cookie cups
sweets
lollipop
biscuit man/gingerbread man

1. Cover margarine container with aluminium foil.
·2. For wheels stick round biscuits to the body with royal icing.
3. Stick an edible cookie cup to the front of the car.
4. Stick two round sweets beside the cookie cup for lights.

5. Fill body of the car with sweets, then push a lollipop into the sweets for a steering wheel.
6. A gingerbread man, if available, can be put behind the steering wheel.

Cot

empty margarine container
cloth or lace
glue
lollipop
fondant
popcorn

1. Wash and dry margarine container thoroughly.
2. Use cloth or lace as wide as the depth of container and tack it with a sewing machine. Glue it to the top of the container.
3. Make a baby from a lollipop and fondant icing as described on p. 7.
4. Fill the cot with pink or white popcorn and let the baby lie on it.

Bags

Lucky dip

Draw a picture on or stick one to a brown-paper or butter-paper bag and fill it with sweets. Fold up at the top.

A lucky dip and bag man
(turn page for instructions).

Hint
On his birthday the child could take a tray of 'baboon bags' to school, with a banana per bag for each of his friends.

Baboon

Fill a bag with sweets and fold it up at the top. Draw a baboon's face, tail and legs on paper, cut out and staple to the paper bag.

Bag man

Draw a cute face and limbs on paper (see figure above), colour the parts in and cut out. Fill a plastic bag with popcorn or other goodies and staple the head and limbs to it.

Rag doll

Fill a paper bag with sweets and fold it up at the top. Draw a doll's face on a round piece of cardboard and stick a paper doilie to it as a bonnet. Cut arms and legs out of the same type of cardboard and staple the parts to the paper bag.

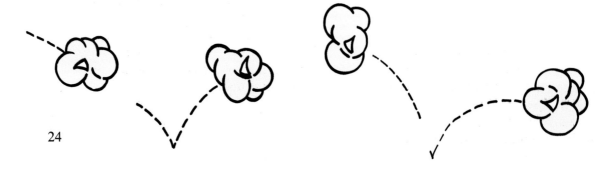

Meringues, jelly and popcorn

Meringues

Meringue mixture

2 egg whites
420 g (500 ml) castor sugar
50 ml boiling water
10 ml white vinegar or lemon juice
5 ml vanilla essence
10 ml baking powder, sifted

1. Mix the egg whites, castor sugar, boiling water, vinegar and vanilla essence in a bowl and beat it for 8 to 10 minutes with an electric mixer until stiff.
2. Fold in the sifted baking powder.
3. Sprinkle a baking sheet with cornflour, or use waxed paper, to prevent the meringues from sticking.
4. Use a star-tipped piping tube in a piping bag. Fill the bag with the mixture and pipe the meringues onto the baking sheet.
5. Bake for 60 minutes at 100°C, turn off oven and leave the meringues in the oven to cool.

Hints
1. Place empty piping bag into an empty jug and fold the top edge of the bag over the top of the jug so that the bag remains upright while filling.
2. Meringues can be frozen.
3. To determine whether there are enough egg whites, break them into a cup. You need a quarter of a cup to absorb the castor sugar sufficiently.

Coloured meringues

basic meringue recipe (see above)
colouring (pink, green and yellow)
strawberry, peppermint and pineapple or
  banana essence
500 ml fresh cream
hundreds and thousands (optional)

1. Divide mixture into three equal parts.
2. Add pink colouring to the first part and flavour it with strawberry essence.
3. Add green colouring to the second and flavour with peppermint essence.
4. Add yellow colouring to the third and flavour it with pineapple or banana essence.
5. Bake meringues as described above.
6. Beat the fresh cream until stiff.
7. Stick meringues to one another in pairs, using the cream.
8. Hundreds and thousands can be sprinkled over the meringues before they are stuck together.
9. Pipe little flowers on the meringues, using a star-tipped piping nozzle and cream.
10. If desired, meringues can be placed individually in paper cookie cups to be served on a plate.

Chocolate meringues

2 egg whites
5 ml lemon juice or white vinegar
200 g (240 ml) castor sugar, sifted
a pinch of salt
5 ml icing sugar, sifted
90 g dark milk chocolate, melted

1. Mix the egg whites, lemon juice and salt and beat for 15 minutes with an electric mixer at the highest speed.
2. Fold in sifted icing sugar.
3. Spoon the mixture into a piping bag and pipe the meringues onto a prepared baking sheet.
4. Bake for 60 minutes at 100°C, switch off and leave to cool in the oven.
5. Dip the point of each meringue into the melted chocolate.

Hints
1. Meringues become soft if stuck together with cream for too long. A safe time is about half an hour before serving.
2. The basic meringue recipe can also be used to make the following shapes and figures: mice, snails, hedgehogs, nests and names.

Examples of the uses
of jelly.

Jelly

Jelly bowls

2 packets of jelly in different colours
empty paper ice-cream containers
fresh cream, whipped

1. Prepare jelly according to the instructions on the jelly packet. Prepare the two colours separately.
2. Fill the ice-cream containers halfway with one colour and leave to set; add the second colour on top and leave to set.
3. Fill a piping tube with the whipped cream and decorate the jelly bowls.

Jelly boats

1 packet of jelly, or more if there are many guests
empty margarine containers, cleaned
1 packet wafer biscuits

1. Prepare jelly according to the instructions and leave to cool off. Pour jelly into the margarine containers just before jelly sets. Containers do not have to be completely filled.
2. Leave jelly to set. Just before serving, dip containers into hot water for a count of six, then turn over onto a plate. (Jelly can be left in containers, if desired.)
3. Use wafer biscuits to make sails for the boats.

Jelly mosaic

3 packets of jelly, different colours
edible cookie cups (optional)
ice-cream cones (optional)
ice-cream

1. Prepare jelly according to instructions. Keep the three colours separately in three flat bowls of different sizes.

2. Leave jelly to set, then cut into small blocks.
3. Mix the three colours lightly in a large bowl. Serve in small bowls, cookie cups or ice-cream cones.
4. Add ice-cream on top.

Jelly baskets

oranges
1 packet of orange jelly
carrot(s), cut in small strips
fresh cream, whipped
red cherries

1. Cut oranges in two halves. Squeeze out the juice and remove fibres.
2. Prepare jelly according to instructions, but use half the water indicated and make up the other half with orange juice.
3. Fill empty orange halves with jelly and leave to set.

4. Complete the baskets by adding carrot strips for handles.
5. Pipe a little flower of fresh cream on the jelly and decorate further with a red cherry.

Jelly oranges

1 packet of green jelly
oranges
raisins
green cherries

1. Cut oranges in half. Squeeze out juice and remove fibres.
2. Prepare jelly and fill the empty orange halves, then leave jelly to set.
3. Cut every half jelly orange in two.
4. Serve with raisins and cherries.

Colourful ideas for popcorn (see p. 28 for instructions).

Jelly cars

2 packets of jelly, different colours
car jelly moulds
cocktail sticks
paper flags, each with a child's name written on it
chocolate vermicelli

1. Prepare each packet of jelly separately and pour into moulds; leave to set.
2. Dip the moulds in hot water for a count of six and turn over on plates.
3. Pin the name of each child to a car with a cocktail stick.
4. Sprinkle chocolate vermicelli around the car.

Popcorn

Popcorn animals

115 g (150 ml) sugar
125 ml golden syrup
50 g jelly powder
popped corn (125 ml unpopped corn yields about ten animals)
animal moulds
butter-paper
sweets, including liquorice
cherries

1. Make a syrup from the first three ingredients, stirring over a low temperature until sugar is dissolved. When the mixture starts to boil, stop stirring and leave to boil for 5 minutes. Leave to cool.
2. Pour mixture over the popcorn and stir to cover all the corn with syrup.
3. Place the animal moulds on butter-paper. Fill each one with popcorn and syrup mixture and press down firmly in the mould.
4. Decorate with sweets, liquorice and cherries.

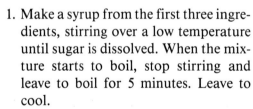

Colourful popcorn

400 g (500 ml) sugar
40 g margarine
75 ml water
essence
colouring
⅓ packet of unpopped corn (prepare to yield about 4 litres of popcorn)

1. Prepare a syrup of the first four ingredients in a deep pan. Stir constantly at a low temperature until boiling starts. Boil for a few minutes until frothy.
2. Take off the stove and add the prepared popcorn. Stir quickly to cover all the popcorn with syrup.
3. Leave to cool and dry.
4. Repeat with the same ingredients, using a different colour.

Popcorn balls

400 g (500 ml) sugar
125 ml water
1 ml cream of tartar
2,5 ml vanilla essence
popcorn

1. Stir all the ingredients except vanilla essence in a stewing pot until the sugar is dissolved.
2. Boil the mixture until it forms a soft ball when tested in cold water. Do not stir.
3. Remove from the stove and add the essence.
4. Pour the syrup over the prepared popcorn.
5. Butter your hands and form balls with the mixture.

More hints

1. String the popcorn pieces on threads of cotton and hang up.
2. String the popcorn balls and use as decoration.
3. Spike popcorn balls on skewers.
4. Pack colourful popcorn balls in cellophane bags or in paper cups.

Salty snacks

Sausages

'vetkoek' dough
sausages
Ready doe or mashed potatoes
    (variation)
cooking oil

1. Prepare the 'vetkoek' dough. Wrap pieces of cut sausage in it.
2. Drop into deep hot cooking oil.
3. A strip of *Ready doe* can also be wrapped around the sausages and then baked in the oven at 180°C. Another variation is to form 12,5 ml of mashed potato in a small ball, then press pieces of cut sausage in it to resemble a hedgehog. Use sausage rings for the eyes.

Cheese fruit

processed cheese wedges
colouring
parsley

1. Mash the cheese wedges.
2. Mix with different colourings.
3. Form into various fruit shapes and decorate with parsley.

Carrot flowers

carrot
orange
cocktail sticks
cheese (optional)

1. Slice across a fairly thick carrot to form circles and cut or nick the edges creating flower shapes.
2. Cut an orange in two halves and put halves upside down on a plate.
3. Stick the cocktail sticks into the orange and impale the flowers on them. Pieces of cheese can be put in between.

Friendly carrot man

carrot
cocktail sticks
raisins
polony
lettuce

1. Cut off the leaves of a medium sized carrot about 100 mm from the carrot body. Cut off the bottom half of the carrot and discard it. The top half is then used as the head.
2. Stick on raisins for the eyes and a piece of polony for the mouth, using the broken-off tips of cocktail sticks.
3. Decorate with parsley.

Cucumber crocodile

cheese
sausages
cocktail sticks
cucumber
almonds
pickled onions
olives (optional)
lettuce

1. Skewer cubes of cheese and sausage on a number of cocktail sticks.
2. Slice through the cucumber sideways from one end up to the middle.
3. Put almonds in the mouth for teeth. Stick in pickled onions or olives cut in half for the eyes.
4. Decorate the back of the crocodile with the skewered cheese and sausage cubes.
5. Shred the lettuce and sprinkle around the crocodile to look like grass.

A variety of salty and sweet snacks: toasted cheese and tomato sandwiches and sliced bread rolls sprinkled with chocolate vermicelli (in the basket) and bread wrapped around pieces of sausage (in front of the cheese and tomato sandwiches on the napkin).

Sandwiches

It is safest to restrict yourself to well known spreads that you know the children like. To make the sandwiches more interesting, you can cut them into various shapes.

1. Mash three bananas and mix with 5 ml sugar and a little lemon juice or peanut butter.
2. Mix cheese and lettuce.
3. Mash hard boiled eggs and mix with mayonnaise. Flavour with a little salt and pepper.
4. Hollow out a French loaf and stuff with one of the above mixtures or flavoursome meat. Slice the bread and serve with lettuce.

Left: In the basket at the back are *Marmite* patties and in the one in front cheese cakes and cheese balls.

31

Coloured eggs, a cucumber crocodile, a friendly carrot man, egg faces and cheese fruit.

1. Boil the eggs until hard.
2. Mix the colouring, vinegar and boiling water.
3. Shell the eggs while still warm. Place in the vinegar mixture and move around until the eggs are coloured.
4. Allow the eggs to dry before arranging on a platter and serving.

Bread pancakes

white bread
margarine
grated biltong
cheese spread (optional)
cocktail stick

1. Cut off the crusts of a slice of white bread. Roll it flat with a rolling pin.
2. Spread with margarine and sprinkle with biltong, or spread with cheese.
3. Roll up like a pancake and pin it down with a cocktail stick.

Bread ship

bread roll
cheese or cheese wedges
cocktail stick
pickled onion

1. Decorate a bread roll with a cheese wedge or a triangle cut from cheese; place it upright using a cocktail stick and a pickled onion.

Egg face

egg, hard boiled
lettuce
cheese spread or mayonnaise
raisins
cheese
tomato
carrot

Hint
Cut white and brown bread in thick slices or blocks and arrange them in the form of a chequer board.

1. Shell a hard-boiled egg and cut in half lengthwise.
2. Place the egg halves upside down on a plate, that is, with the white side upwards.
3. Decorate all around with chopped lettuce.
4. Pipe the eyes, nose, mouth and hair onto egg halves with cheese spread or mayonnaise.
5. Stick on raisins for the eyes, a piece of cheese for the nose and the mouth can be a slice of tomato.
6. Decorate the hair further with pieces of grated carrot.

Coloured eggs

eggs
1 ml colouring (any colour)
37,5 ml vinegar
250 ml boiling water

Salty biscuit boat

salty biscuit
butter or margarine
sweetmilk cheese

1. Spread the salty biscuit with butter or margarine.
2. Cut thin triangular slices from the sweetmilk cheese. Cut each triangle halfway down the middle and fold the edges away from one another.
3. Place the triangle upright on top of the biscuit.

32

Bread car

bread roll
Vienna sausage
polony
cocktail sticks

1. Hollow out a bread roll.
2. Make a manikin from half a Vienna sausage and place inside.
3. Cut polony slices for the wheels and affix them with cocktail sticks; affix another carrot slice for the steering wheel.

Bread dog

bread roll
meat stuffing
polony
pickled onions or cheese

1. Hollow out the bread roll.
2. Fill it with any meat stuffing.
3. Make ears with polony, and the nose and eyes with pickled onions or pieces of cheese.

Spider or crab

'vetkoek' mixture and cooking oil
Nik-naks
cottage cheese

1. Prepare the 'vetkoek' mixture and drop teaspoonsful into deep hot cooking oil.
2. When cool, cut a groove into each side, using a sharp knife. Insert the ends of two or more *Nik-Naks* in each groove.
3. Make two eyes in front (in the centre) with cottage cheese.

Rainbow snacks

bread
margarine or butter
colouring

It is not advisable to prepare exotic fillings for a children's party. Butter of various colours is much more important.

1. Cut thin bread slices. Spread with margarine or butter of various colours and sandwich together in layers. Cut off the crusts.
2. Wrap tightly and refrigerate.
3. Cut into various shapes.

Butter can also be coloured and flavoured with tomato sauce, parsley, and *Marmite*. Blue, red, pink, yellow or green vegetable colouring can also be used.

Biltong snacks

bread
margarine or butter
Marmite
finely grated biltong

1. Cut one thick slice of bread at a time. Cut off the crusts.
2. Cut the slice into six blocks or squares.
3. Mix *Marmite* with margarine or butter. Spread the bread blocks on all sides.
4. Roll in grated biltong.

Biltong marbles

yolks of 3 hard-boiled eggs
225 g cottage cheese
biltong, grated

Biltong snacks, carrot flowers, a bread car, bread ship, rainbow snacks, bread dogs and bread pancakes.

33

1. Rub the yolks through a sieve and mix thoroughly with cottage cheese.
2. Form small balls the size of marbles and roll them in the grated biltong.
3. Place in refrigerator for 2 hours. Serve on cocktail sticks.

Cheese rolls

1 white or brown bread, sliced thinly
110 g butter or margarine, melted
110 g (250 ml) cheese, grated

1. Pre-heat the oven to 200°C.
2. Cut off the crusts. Roll each slice flat with a rolling pin.
3. Coat bread with the melted butter or margarine, sprinkle with cheese and roll up.
4. Put the rolls on a baking sheet and coat with butter or margarine again.
5. Bake for 10 minutes, turn over, coat with the remaining shortening and bake until very crisp and golden brown. Serve warm.

Cheese balls

250 ml mashed potatoes
250 g (250 ml) Cheddar cheese, grated
1 egg
60 g (125 ml) cake flour
3 ml baking powder
a pinch of salt
a pinch of pepper
a pinch of paprika
parsley to taste

1. Mix all the ingredients together thoroughly. Form small balls.
2. Drop into deep cooking oil and fry until golden brown.

Marmite patties

140 g (250 ml) cake flour
5 ml baking powder
a pinch of red pepper
2,5 ml salt
125 g butter or margarine, grated

375 g (375 ml) strong Cheddar cheese, grated
1 large egg
125 ml milk
37,5 ml butter or margarine
5 ml *Marmite*

1. Sift together all dry ingredients. Add grated butter or margarine.
2. Add the grated cheese and rub in with the fingertips to obtain a crumbly mixture.
3. Beat the egg and milk together and stir into mixture with a fork.
4. Spoon the pastry into a greased pan.
5. Bake at 160°C until light brown.
6. Slowly melt shortening and *Marmite* together and pour over the warm patties.
7. Serve up warm.
8. The mixture yields about 5 dozen.

Cheese cakes

500 g cake flour
3 ml salt
pinch of red pepper
500 g Cheddar cheese
500 g butter (gives better results than margarine)
1 egg yolk
Marmite
a little margarine and *Fondor*

1. Sift together dry ingredients.
2. Grate the cheese and butter in with the flour mixture. Using hands, mix thoroughly to a stiff, smooth dough.
3. For better results, dough can be placed in a plastic bag and refrigerated overnight.
4. Roll out the dough thinly and press out shapes with a biscuit cutter.
5. Place in an ungreased pan (there is enough butter in the dough).
6. Use a small brush to daub egg yolk mixed with water over the cakes.
7. Bake for about 6 minutes at 200°C until nicely yellow.
8. Allow to cool and stick together in pairs, using *Marmite* mixed with margarine and a little *Fondor*.

Sweet snacks

Cup and saucer

ice-cream cone
royal icing
Marie biscuit
marshmallow
butter icing

1. Cut off the top section of an ice-cream cone at the ridge. Also cut off a small circular strip to be used later for the cup's handle. Stick the top section of the cone on top of the *Marie* biscuit using royal icing. Do the same for the 'handle' of the 'cup'.
2. Place the marshmallow inside the cup and decorate with butter icing around the edge.

Fashion doll

cookie cup
ice-cream cone
royal icing
Marie biscuit
marshmallow
butter icing
sequins
colouring
paper doily

1. First make a hat for the doll as described on p. 37.
2. Cut off a 20 mm strip from the top of the cone and discard.
3. Stick the remaining part of the cone onto a *Marie* biscuit, cut side down, using royal icing.
4. Stick the marshmallow at the top of the cone for the head.
5. Decorate all around the neck with butter icing using a piping tube.
6. Use two round sequins for eyes, and paint on the nose and mouth with a fine brush and vegetable colouring. Allow to dry.

A frog, basket, tea cup and saucer (above), a fashion doll and a clown (left), all made from ice-cream cones and cookie cups.

7. Place hat at a jaunty angle on the doll's head.
8. Cut paper doily to size as a frill around the doll's neck.

Rocket

ice-cream cone
royal icing
Marie biscuit
wafer biscuit
butter icing
sequins (optional)

1. Stick the cone to a *Marie* biscuit with royal icing.

35

Above: Marshmallow ice-cream and marshmallow cups.
Right: A hat, a beetle and a clock.

3. Decorate with butter icing and a piping tube.
4. *Smarties* or other sweets can be used to decorate it further.

Frog

2 cookie cups
Marie biscuit
butter icing
sweets
small marshmallows
vegetable colouring

1. Stick the bottom of one of the cookie cups to the *Marie* biscuit with butter icing. Now stick the second cookie cup upside down onto the first at a slight angle to form an open mouth.
2. Fill the mouth with sweets.
3. Make eyes with marshmallows.
4. Decorate around the bottom with butter icing using a piping tube.

Marshmallow ice-cream

marshmallows
ice-cream cones
hundreds and thousands

1. Melt a quantity of marshmallows according to the number of children.
2. Fill an ice-cream cone to the top with the marshmallow mixture and allow to cool.
3. Sprinkle the hundreds and thousands on top.

Marshmallow cup

marshmallows
cookie cups
hundreds and thousands

1. Melt enough marshmallows according to the number of children.
2. Fill the cookie cups to the top with the marshmallow mixture and allow to cool. Sprinkle the hundreds and thousands on top.

2. Slit the wafer biscuit diagonally (see photograph on p. 37) and stick three fins against the cone with royal icing.
3. Decorate the rocket further using butter icing in a piping tube.
4. Sequins can be pressed into the butter icing around the edges of the fins.

Windmill

ice-cream cone
Marie biscuit
royal icing
wafer biscuit
butter icing
Smarties or other small round sweets (optional)

1. Stick the cone to a *Marie* biscuit with royal icing.
2. Cut the wafer biscuit lengthwise in half and stick the two parts crosswise to the cone, about 20 mm from the top, to form the windmill vanes.

36

Fruit basket

cookie cup
sweets
liquorice
royal icing and butter icing

1. Fill the cookie cup with brightly coloured sweets.
2. Make a handle for the basket with a strip of liquorice. Stick it on with royal icing.
3. Decorate the edges of the basket with butter icing.

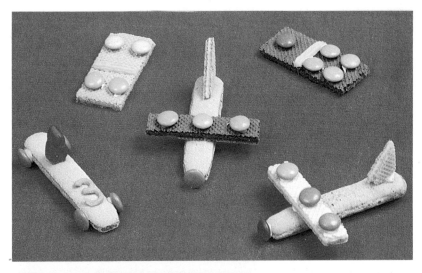

Hat

Marie biscuit
cookie cup
butter icing

1. Spread butter icing on the *Marie* biscuit and smooth.
2. Place the cookie cup upside down on top.
3. Decorate the edge of the cookie cup and tie a bow around the hat. Place a flower in the bow.

Above: A racing car, dominoes and aeroplanes.
Left: A windmill and a rocket.

Clock

Marie biscuit
butter icing, brightly coloured and plain

1. Spread plain butter icing smoothly on the *Marie* biscuit.
2. Write on the numbers and hands with coloured icing in a piping tube.

Dominoes

biscuit
butter icing, chocolate
silver balls or *Jelly Tots*

1. Use any rectangular biscuit.
2. Spread butter icing (chocolate or any other colour) on the biscuit.
3. Make the dots with silver balls or *Jelly Tots*.

Aeroplane

finger biscuit and wafers
royal icing
Smarties

1. Use the whole finger biscuit and half a wafer. With royal icing stick the wafer crosswise to the finger biscuit to form the aeroplane's wing.
2. Stick on a triangle from another wafer for the tailpiece.
3. Decorate with *Smarties*.

Clown

ice-cream cone
sweets
royal icing
Marie biscuit
marshmallow
lollipop (optional)
Smarties

37

Bread cakes (right) and biscuit faces (far right).

1. Take a finger biscuit and stick on four *Smarties* with royal icing to form the wheels (any other round, hard sweets can also be used).
2. Stick a jelly baby on the biscuit, standing it upright.
3. Write a number on the car with a piping tube.
4. Use two silver balls for the lights at the front.

Bread cakes

white bread
biscuit cutter
butter or margarine
chocolate vermicelli
hundreds and thousands

1. Slice the bread and press out various shapes with a biscuit cutter.
2. Spread with margarine or butter and sprinkle with chocolate vermicelli or hundreds and thousands.

1. Cut off the tip of the cone and set aside. Place sweets inside the remaining cone.
2. Cover the large rim of the cone with royal icing and stick it onto the *Marie* biscuit.
3. Affix a marshmallow to the smaller open tip of the cone, or stick a round lollipop into it.
4. Decorate the lollipop's face and hair with royal icing.
5. The tip of the cone (cut off earlier) can be stuck on top as a hat.
6. Decorate further with *Smarties*.

A smaller clown can be made in the same way by cutting off more of the cone. Only a face, without the body, can be made using a marshmallow.

Lollipop

lollipop
hundreds and thousands

1. Take off the lollipop wrapper and wipe lightly with a clean, damp cloth.
2. Dip the lollipop in hundreds and thousands.

Racing car

finger biscuit
Smarties
royal icing
jelly baby
silver balls

Beetle

paper cookie cup
butter icing
Smarties
liquorice

1. Spread the paper cookie cup with dark pink butter icing.
2. Make spots with brown icing or brown *Smarties*.
3. Use strips of liquorice for the feelers.

Flower

marshmallow
jelly crystals or hundreds and
    thousands
Smarties
royal icing
green paper (optional)

1. Cut petals from the marshmallow using a pair of scissors. Form the flower.
2. Sprinkle with jelly crystals or hundreds and thousands.
3. Put a *Smartie* in the flower's centre.
4. Leaves of green paper can be made.

Biscuit faces

royal icing
pink essence
colouring
Marie biscuit

1. Prepare the royal icing, adding a little pink essence and colouring. Spread on the *Marie* biscuit.
2. Decorate as desired (see photograph on p. 38).

Lollipop faces

lollipops
stiff paper
glue

1. Use a variety of lollipops.
2. Draw faces on stiff paper and cut out. Leave the wrapping on the lollipops and glue on the faces.
3. Decorate further with bows, etc.

Chocolate tea cakes

250 g margarine or butter
250 ml milk
800 g (1 000 ml) sugar
100 g (250 ml) cocoa
450 to 540 g (5 to 6 x 250 ml) oats
160 g (500 ml) desiccated coconut
10 ml vanilla essence

Lollipop faces.

39

1. Cook the first four ingredients together for 5 minutes, then remove from the stove.
2. Add oats, coconut and vanilla essence. Stir well until thoroughly mixed.
3. Spoon the mixture out in balls on a greased surface.

'Rice Krispie' ice-cream balls

20 g margarine
10 marshmallows
½ pack *Rice Krispies*
ice-cream cones or skewers

1. Melt the margarine and marshmallows together. Add the *Rice Krispies* and mix well.
2. Form a ball and place in the ice-cream cone, or string a few on a skewer.

Sugar moulds

Cakes can be decorated with a variety of mouldings made with sugar. The moulds are available commercially.

210 g (250 ml) castor sugar
15 ml water
colouring (optional)

1. Mix the castor sugar and water. Add a little colouring, if desired.
2. Press down the sugar firmly into the mould. Unmould on a flat surface. Leave to dry for half a day.
3. Colouring can be painted on with a brush.

'Sinatjies' (cup-cakes)

250 g margarine or butter
300 g (375 ml) sugar
5 eggs
420 g (750 ml) self-raising flour
2 ml salt
2 ml vanilla essence
990 g (750 ml) smooth apricot jam
250 ml water
240 g (750 ml) desiccated coconut

1. Set oven to 190°C. Grease pattypans with margarine.
2. Cream shortening and sugar. Add eggs.
3. Add dry ingredients and vanilla essence.
4. Spoon into pans. Bake for 15 minutes until golden brown.
5. Meanwhile, heat the apricot jam and water to boiling point.
6. Dunk the cup-cakes with a skimmer into the hot syrup one by one. Lift out and roll in the coconut.

Decorated butter-biscuits

240 g margarine
100 g (125 ml) sugar
vanilla essence
360 g (750 ml) cake flour
liquorice (optional)
Jelly Tots (optional)
hundreds and thousands (optional)

1. Mix margarine, sugar and essence and work in the flour.
2. Roll out 12 mm thick on a plank lightly sprinkled with flour.
3. Cut or press various shapes from the dough.
4. Decorate with liquorice, *Jelly Tots* and hundreds and thousands. Bake at 180°C until light brown.

Chocolate crackling

190 g (375 ml) icing sugar
40 g (100 ml) cocoa
80 g (250 ml) desiccated coconut
4 x 250 ml *Rice Krispies*
250 g butter or margarine

1. Sift icing sugar and cocoa into a large mixing bowl.
2. Add the coconut to the *Rice Krispies* and mix it with the cocoa and icing sugar.
3. Melt the shortening and add to dry ingredients.
4. Mix well.
5. Spoon into a pattypan and leave in the refrigerator to set.

Honey snacks

60 g butter
50 ml honey
10 g (12 ml) sugar
4 x 250 ml corn flakes
90 g (150 ml) shelled peanuts, unsalted

1. Put the butter, honey and sugar into a pan. Stir at a low temperature until the butter is melted.
2. Mix the corn flakes and peanuts in a bowl. Pour over the honey and butter mixture. Mix until the corn flakes and peanuts are thoroughly covered by the syrup.
3. Spoon mixture into paper cups placed in a pan.
4. Bake for 8 minutes in a medium oven, remove and leave to cool for 15 minutes.
5. The ingredients yield about 30 snacks.

Melt-in-the-mouth marshmallows

260 g (500 ml) castor sugar
125 ml cold water
30 ml gelatine
100 ml hot water
2 ml pink colouring (or any other colour)
flavouring
desiccated coconut for decoration

1. Put castor sugar and cold water into a mixing bowl and beat at high speed with an electric mixer.
2. Dissolve the gelatine in hot water and add to the sugar mixture. Beat for about 15 minutes until the mixture is thick.
3. Add colouring and flavouring.
4. Pour the mixture into a flat, greased bowl and leave in the refrigerator to set.
5. Cut the marshmallows into squares and roll in desiccated coconut.

Biscuit names

180 g (325 ml) cake flour
5 ml baking powder
5 ml salt
270 g soft margarine or butter
200 g (250 ml) sugar
2 eggs
5 ml vanilla or lemon essence
1 egg yolk
1,5 ml water
colouring

1. Set the oven to 200°C.
2. Sift cake flour, baking powder and salt together.
3. Beat shortening, sugar, eggs and flavouring until creamy. Add the flour mixture and mix very well.
4. Let cool for an hour or till the dough is easily manageable.
5. Take a quarter of the dough and roll it out on a plank sprinkled with flour; leave the rest of the dough in the refrigerator. Press out shapes with a biscuit cutter and place on a greased baking sheet.
6. Mix the egg yolk and water with a fork and add vegetable colouring.
7. Using a paint brush or cotton wool wound tightly around a thin stick, paint a name or the letters of the alphabet onto the biscuits.
8. Bake for 6 to 8 minutes or until done, but not brown.
9. Roll out the remainder of the dough, decorate and bake.

Marshmallow animals

25 ml icing sugar
marshmallow

1. Mix the marshmallow and icing sugar by kneading the mixture to a dough.
2. Mould any animal with this mixture.
3. For larger quantities use more icing sugar and marshmallows. Be careful not to mix too large a quantity at one time.

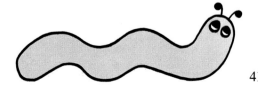

Bread cakes

Above: The completed train.
Right: The forming of the locomotive.
Below: The forming of the carriages.

Train

1 white or brown loaf
butter mixture, e.g. Cheddar cheese and
  butter
8 Vienna sausages
16 round salty biscuits
lettuce
8 square salty biscuits
½ carrot
parsley

1. Cut loaf in two. Use the larger part for
   the train's rear (see third figure) and use
   two thick slices for the carriages.
2. Prepare butter mixture and spread it
   over two pieces of the locomotive as
   well as the carriages. Join the locomotive's pieces as shown in sketch.
3. Stick the sausages, biscuits and lettuce
   to the train using the butter mixture.
4. Use a knife to make a small hole at the
   front of the locomotive and stick the
   half carrot into it.
5. Decorate train all around with parsley,
   lettuce, etc.

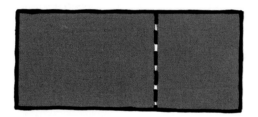

Flowers

lettuce
1 hard-boiled egg
8 slices of bread, 10 mm thick
200 g (220 ml) soft butter
1 packet of hundreds and thousands
yellow and pink colouring
rhubarb stalks, or any other vegetable
  stalks
small spinach leaves
cubes of tomato and cheese, radishes and
  parsley for decoration

1. Slice lettuce and sprinkle on a large
   round tray or a round board covered
   with foil.
2. Cut egg in half and place in position on
   tray.

3. Cut bread in a petal shape (see photograph on p. 38).
4. Add colouring to butter and spread on bread.
5. Sprinkle hundreds and thousands over petals to make the flower even more attractive.
6. Arrange four petals around each egg half and give each flower a green stem; use spinach as leaves for the flowers.
7. Decorate edge of the tray or board with tomato and cheese cubes or radishes with pieces of parsley in between.

Egg dumpties

3 eggs
mashed potato mixture or cheese spread
  (see recipe on p. 34)
1 loaf of bread
vegetable colouring
parsley
thin bread sticks
coloured pickled onions
peanuts and raisins

1. Boil eggs until hard.
2. Colour mashed potatoes with a few drops of chocolate colouring.
3. Remove crusts, then spread whole loaf with the mashed potatoes or cheese spread.
4. Shell eggs and soak for five minutes in a mixture of 5 ml vegetable colouring in 250 ml water. Cut off one centimetre at the bottom of each egg; keep the off-cuts.
5. Place the three eggs evenly spaced on the top of the loaf.
6. Place the cut-off pieces of egg upside down onto the eggs; they are the dumpties' hats (see illustration above right). Pieces of parsley can be stuck into the hats.
7. Use bread sticks for legs.
8. Decorate the loaf further with pickled onions and parsley.
9. Cover the plate with peanuts and raisins.
10. Make mouths with pieces from the white of the eggs and the eyes with bits of polony.

The egg dumpties sitting on a wall of bread, 'plastered' with cheese spread.

House

2 white or brown loaves
butter mixture or mashed potato mixture
  (see p. 34)
colouring
30 Vienna sausages
square salty biscuits
pickled onion
cheese wedges
radishes
carrots
celery
lettuce, sliced finely
parsley
1 thin roll of French polony

43

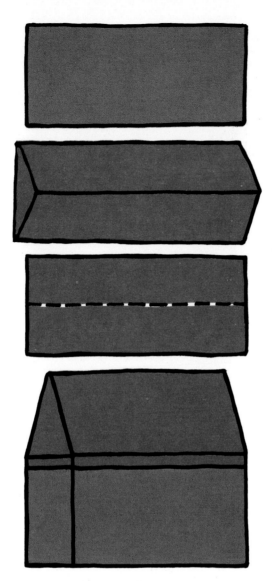

1. Use one loaf for the walls of the house by cutting two equal strips lengthwise (see third figure).
2. Cut the other loaf diagonally to form the roof.
3. Prepare butter or mashed potato mixture and colour as desired with a few drops of colouring.
4. Spread the two halves of the first loaf with the butter mixture or potato mixture and sandwich together.
5. Stick on the roof with the butter or potato mixture.
6. Coat the outside of the house with the mixture and decorate the bottom edges with carrot flowers and Vienna slices (see photograph below).
7. Cut sausages lengthwise and place alongside one another on both sides of the roof to look like tiles.
8. Use the square salty biscuits for windows and make a door with polony. Use cheese wedges for a wall around the house. The door knob is a pickled onion.
9. Make flowers from the carrots, radishes and parsley. Use sliced lettuce for the lawn.
10. Impale celery on a cocktail stick for trees and press the stick into a thick slice of polony.
11. Finish off as prepared.

A house that is completely edible − from its door knob (a pickled onion) to its roof tiles (sliced sausages).

Bread faces.

Bread faces (serves two)

1 round bread roll
lettuce
carrots
margarine
vegetable colouring
1 Vienna sausage
2 serviettes (blue or pink)
grated cheese

1. Cut bread roll in half. Chop the lettuce finely and dry. Cut carrots into thin slices.
2. Mix a few drops of pink colouring with the margarine and spread the bread rolls.
3. Slice sausage in rings and use for eyes and nose. Use a half circle for the mouth.
4. Fold the serviettes in a triangle and place each on a side plate with the point towards you. Place each roll on a serviette (see photograph).
5. Sprinkle grated cheese on each roll for hair. Decorate the roll around the bottom with the carrot strips and lettuce.

An assortment of butter mixtures and salty spreads

1. Cream cheese mixed with cheese spread.
2. Margarine mixed with *Marmite*.
3. Cream cheese mixed with tomato sauce and mashed hard-boiled egg.
4. Margarine mixed with finely grated Cheddar cheese.
5. Mashed potato mixed with a little butter, tomato sauce or *Fondor*, etc.

Quick-and-easy cakes

The following recipes are for a cake base for birthday cakes. All are proven and can be cut and coated easily.

Boiled milk sponge cake (basic recipe)

60 g butter or margarine
250 ml milk
3 to 4 eggs
375 g (470 ml) sugar
250 g (520 ml) cake flour
4 x 5 ml baking powder
pinch of salt

1. Use two round cake tins about 230 mm in diameter. Trace exact size of the pans on waxed paper and cut out two circles to put on the bottom of the pans. Grease sides with margarine.
2. Bring shortening and milk to the boil.
3. Beat the eggs and sugar until the sugar is dissolved.
4. Sift cake flour and baking powder together and add a pinch of salt. Fold in flour mixture with egg mixture.
5. Add the milk little by little to the egg-and-flour mixture, blend thoroughly and pour into cake tins.
6. Bake for about 20 minutes at 180°C.

Chocolate cake

6 eggs, whites and yolks separated
240 g (500 ml) cake flour
400 g (500 ml) sugar
pinch of salt
250 ml cooking oil
125 ml cocoa
250 ml boiling water
4 x 5 ml baking powder

1. Line two cake tins with waxed paper and grease sides with margarine.
2. Beat the egg whites until stiff — keep aside.
3. Beat remaining ingredients together, except baking powder.
4. Lastly add the baking powder and whisked egg whites.
5. Bake for about 20 minutes at 190°C.

Easy rainbow cake

1 x recipe for *Boiled milk sponge cake*
colouring

1. Prepare the batter, divide in two or three parts and add a few drops of colouring to each part.
2. Mix well and pour the different colours together in two prepared cake tins.
3. Bake as indicated for the boiled milk sponge cake.

The above recipes can be used in the following designs:

Train

cake mix
blue butter icing
liquorice shoelaces
white popcorn
plastic train carriages, one for each year of the child's age

1. Bake a round layer cake.
2. Place one layer of the cake on a round cake dish. Spread icing on top and sandwich the second layer.
3. Coat the whole cake with blue butter icing.
4. Using liquorice shoelaces make a train track around the top edge of the cake.
5. Heap popcorn in the middle of the cake to represent coal.
6. Place plastic carriages on the track.
7. Use a star-tipped piping tube to decorate bottom edge of the cake with butter icing.

Horse race

cake mix
white butter icing or frosting
sugar horses
vegetable colouring
liquorice shoelaces and *Jelly Tots*

1. Bake a round cake. Coat with white butter icing or frosting.
2. Make horse-shaped sugar mouldings. (Any plastic mould that can be used for chocolate, clay or sugar is suitable – see p. 40 for an explanation of the use of sugar mouldings).
3. Use vegetable colouring and paint the horses various colours. Arrange them upright all along the top edge of the cake.
4. Tie liquorice shoelaces around the neck of each horse and bring them all together at the centre of the cake.
5. Decorate the cake around the top and bottom with *Jelly Tots*.

Rice paper decoration

cake mix
butter icing
a sheet of rice paper (obtainable at shops selling cake decorations)
a picture to copy onto the cake
pencil
jelly piping

1. Bake a square or round cake. Coat with butter icing.
2. Trace the picture with a pencil onto the rice paper (it is edible but tasteless), then trace the outline with jelly piping (this prevents the colours from flowing when the picture is coloured in).

3. Colour in the picture with vegetable colouring.
4. Place it on top of the decorated cake.

Monkey on a barrel

cake mix
2 jam tins
butter icing
colouring (brown and green)
picture of a monkey (cardboard)
desiccated coconut

1. Bake cake mix in two jam tins and remove from tins when cool.
2. Colour butter icing brown. Spread one end of each cake with icing and sandwich together to form the barrel.
3. Decorate round the bottom with a piping tube, and also decorate the sides of the barrel.
4. Place the monkey on top.
5. Mix a few drops of green vegetable colouring well with the coconut and sprinkle around the barrel.

Clown party

cake mix
butter icing
colouring (brown and yellow)
7 fondant clowns (see p. 7)
balloons

1. Bake a round cake.
2. Divide butter icing in half. Colour one half brown and the other yellow. Decorate the cake with brown icing. Pipe on big yellow stars with a piping tube to mark the places where the clowns will be placed.
3. Place the clowns on the stars, then decorate the cake round the bottom with more yellow stars.
4. Decorate cake further with balloons. Use a little icing to prevent the balloons from rolling off.

Drum

cake mix
butter icing
brown colouring
silver balls
Smarties
2 round lollipops, wrapped
2 drinking straws
crinkle paper

1. Bake a round cake and coat it with butter icing coloured light brown. Decorate stars around the top and bottom edges of the drum cake.
2. Decorate the top edge with silver balls and arrange *Smarties* in a zig-zag pattern around the side of the cake.
3. For drum sticks insert lollipops into the two drinking straws. Glue the end of a strip of brightly coloured crinkle paper to the end of each lollipop and wrap the paper around it.
4. Place the two drum sticks on top of the drum.
5. More lollipops can be arranged around the cake.

Dog

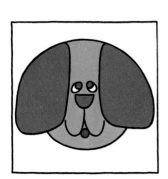

cake mix
butter icing
brown colouring
brown cardboard or painted cardboard
1 marshmallow (white), cut in half
2 brown *Smarties*
1 brown wafer
liquorice shoelaces

1. Bake a round single layer cake and coat with butter icing coloured light brown.
2. Cut ears from cardboard and stick them to the head.
3. Use marshmallow for the dog's eyes and stick a brown *Smartie* on each eye.
4. Use the wafer and liquorice for the nose, mouth, whiskers and tail.

Lion

cake mix
butter icing, coloured yellow
crinkle paper (orange)
2 *Lemon Creams*
Smarties
1 *Romany Cream*

1. Bake a round single layer cake and coat with yellow butter icing.
2. Gather a strip of crinkle paper to fit around the cake to form the mane.
3. Pipe icing around the bottom of the cake as well as just above the mane.
4. Press the *Lemon Creams* for ears into the cake and put on the *Romany Cream* for the nose, then decorate the face further as desired.

Elephant

cake mix
butter icing, coloured pink
cardboard
Smarties

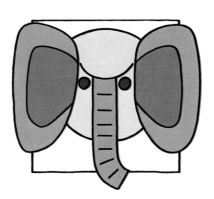

1. Bake a round single layer cake and coat it with pink butter icing.
2. Cut the ears and trunk from cardboard and paint them grey. Stick in *Smarties* for the eyes.
3. Fix the ears and trunk to the cake. To prevent them from falling over pipe icing in front of and behind the ears.

Red Indian

cake mix
butter icing
plastic feathers, or feathers cut from cardboard
Smarties (red and yellow)

1. Bake a round cake and coat it with white butter icing.
2. Paint diagonal stripes on the 'face' using a brush and vegetable colouring.
3. Place feathers around the Red Indian's head and decorate it at the 'throat' with yellow and red *Smarties*.

Pirate

cake mix
butter icing
black cardboard
chocolate biscuit
Smarties and liquorice shoelaces

1. Bake a round single layer cake and coat it with white butter icing.
2. Make a hat of cardboard for the pirate as shown in the figure below.
3. Use a *Smartie* for one eye; the eyepatch for the other eye is a chocolate biscuit and its string is made of liquorice.

Ice-cream cakes

There are various ways in which ordinary sorbet or vanilla ice-cream can be made more attractive for a children's party.

For instance, cut marshmallows, cherries or nuts into pieces and mix these pieces into the ice-cream. If preferred, add 2,5 ml rose essence per 2 litres of ice-cream. Mix well, scoop into a suitable mould and place in the deep-freeze.

For modelling purposes white commercial ice-cream may be coloured as desired and refrozen in an enamel container. Use this layer of ice-cream as, for example, cycle-track, rugby-field, skating rink or farmyard and decorate it with chocolate vermicelli, coloured coconut, jelly which is available in plastic tubes and plastic figures or figures made of fondant or instant plastic icing (see pp. 7 and 8). The photo on p. 51 gives a few examples of the uses of fondant or instant plastic icing.

To make ice-cream faces, spoon balls of ice-cream onto a plate and decorate it with wafers, *Jelly Tots* and ice-cream cones (see example on p. 50). Prepare the necessary ears, eyes, bows, etc. before the time and do the final decoration just before serving. Jelly can be placed around the faces.

49

Far right: A few examples of the figures that could be made of fondant or instant plastic icing.

Right: A block of vanilla ice-cream (any other flavour may also be used), decorated with all kinds of confectionery and 'ice-cream kisses'. Diced jelly could be used for further decoration.

Below: The farmyard on the plate in the middle of the table is 'fenced in' with *Flakes* and finger biscuits, while green jelly forms the grass. On the small plates are a variety of ice-cream faces.

Composite cakes

Kite

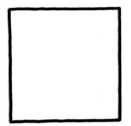

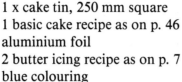

1 x cake tin, 250 mm square
1 basic cake recipe as on p. 46
aluminium foil
2 butter icing recipe as on p. 7
blue colouring
9 small round lollipops
2 *Marie* biscuits – coated with butter icing
3 red jelly beans for the nose
1 large packet of *Jelly Tots*
liquorice
1 packet of *Smarties*
1 packet of wafers

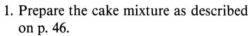

1. Prepare the cake mixture as described on p. 46.
2. Grease the cake tin or cut waxed paper the size of the tin to cover the bottom.
3. Bake as described and leave to cool on a wire tray.
4. Find a base for the cake – a tray, plank, etc. Cover it with aluminium foil to serve as the sky.
5. Prepare butter icing, add blue colouring and coat the background.
6. Cut the cake as shown on the sketch and coat with icing.
7. Decorate the cake as shown on the photograph below left.

Hints
1. *Coat the* Marie *biscuit eyes with butter icing beforehand.*
2. *Press the lollipops into the cake, handle and all.*
3. *Remove the lollipop wrapping only an hour or so before the party as the lollipops tend to melt and drip.*
4. *Cut the wafer as shown with a sharp-toothed knife.*

Lion

1 round cake tin, approximately 225 mm in diameter
½ basic cake recipe as on p. 46
crinkle paper, 1 420 mm x 100 mm, yellow and orange
1 butter icing recipe (p. 7), orange or brown
2 liquorice sweets
1 wafer
salty sticks
liquorice shoelaces

1. Follow the basic cake preparation as described on p. 46.
2. Place the two colours of crinkle paper on top of each other and staple or pin together. Gather in the paper to a length of 710 mm.
3. Cover the lion's face with orange/brown butter icing.
4. Fit the tacked paper around the top edge of the cake.

5. Pipe icing with a star-tipped tube around the border of the cake and paper.
6. Complete the face with the remaining ingredients.

Hints
1. Remember that the icing contains butter, and therefore it will discolour the paper if left too long.
2. The full cake mixture can be prepared and be baked in two cake tins. Only use the one cake.

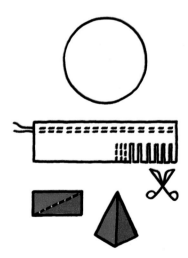

Fish

½ basic cake recipe as on p. 46
1 round cake tin, approximately 225 mm in diameter
2 butter icing recipe as on p. 7, coloured orange

2 packets *Smarties*
1 marshmallow
1 liquorice strip or oblong sweet
10 wafers
coloured oblong sweets for the fins
1 round red lollipop or red cherry

1. Follow the basic preparation of the cake mixture.
2. Cut a strip 50 mm wide through the middle of the cake.
3. Sandwich together the two remaining sections to form the body of the fish.
4. Cut the centre strip as shown for the fins.
5. First coat the fish with orange coloured icing, then the wafers and sweets which are the fins, and push firmly together.
6. Place the *Smarties* in position as scales, each one on its edge.

Hints
1. With a pair of scissors cut the marshmallow in half for the eye, to give a better appearance. Secure it with a small round red lollipop or red cherry.
2. You can use the full cake mixture but bake in two separate tins. Use only one cake for the fish.

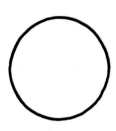

53

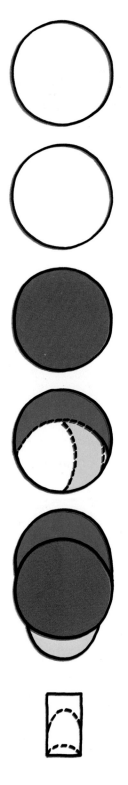

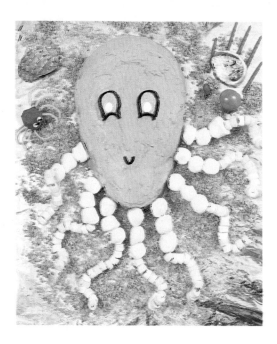

Octopus

1 basic cake recipe as on p. 46
2 round cake tins, 200 mm diameter
2 butter icing recipe as on p. 7
1 packet of large marshmallows
1 packet of small marshmallows
8 lengths florist wire, 270 mm
2 yellow wafers
2 brown *Smarties*
liquorice shoelace

1. Prepare the basic cake mixture as described.
2. Cut the cake as shown in the illustrations. A small piece of cake will be left over.
3. Arrange the cake pieces to form the octopus's head and coat with butter icing, coloured greyish-green.
4. String firstly some large marshmallows on the florist wire and finish with smaller ones.
5. Place these 'tentacles' against the body.
6. Cut the wafers as shown for eyes and decorate.

Hints
Coat the insides of the cake pieces with icing to help them stick together better.

May pole

1 basic cake recipe as on p. 46
2 butter icing recipe as on p. 7, coloured pink
1 long candle
1 doily
2 packets of *Smarties*
4 edible dolls
8 coloured florist ribbons

1. Prepare one basic cake mixture as described.
2. Coat the whole cake with butter icing coloured pink.
3. Cut out a small hole at the centre of the cake for the candle.
4. Place the cake on top of a doily on a plate.
5. Decorate the cake with *Smarties* and use a piping tube to decorate between the sweets.
6. Make a number of edible dolls as described on p. 35.
7. Tie two ribbons for each doll around the top of the candle and place the candle in the centre of the cake.
8. Now decorate around the base of candle, using *Smarties*.
9. Tie one ribbon of each pair to the doll and let the other hang down the candle.

Hints
1. 'Curl' the ribbons with a knife or scissor blade.
2. Instead of making edible dolls icecream cones could be turned upside down and stuck to Marie biscuits with icing. Cut the tips off with a sharp knife, decorate the cones with butter icing and place a birthday candle in each hole.

Bookworm

1 basic cake recipe as on p. 46
3 cake tins, 130 mm diameter
2 butter icing recipe as on p. 7, coloured
   green
½ butter icing recipe as on p. 7, uncoloured
1 orange marshmallow
1 packet of *Smarties*
liquorice shoelaces
muesli
3 *Marie* biscuits
coloured paper for leaves

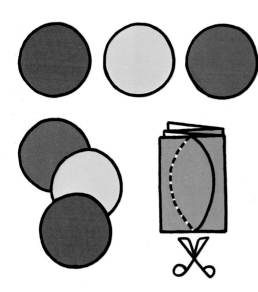

Bee

1 basic cake recipe as on p. 46
4 round cake tins, 130 mm diameter
2 butter icing recipe as on p. 7, coloured
   yellow
1½ butter icing recipe as on p. 7, coloured
   brown
2 brown *Smarties*
1 yellow serviette or a piece of yellow
   paper
4 lengths florist wire, 270 mm
200 g desiccated coconut
2,5 ml green colouring

1. Divide the cake mixture into three equal parts and bake separately in tins 130 mm in diameter.
2. Prepare the base for the cake.
3. Coat each cake individually with green butter icing.
4. Stack the three parts sideways as in photograph above.
5. Using the white icing decorate the face.
6. Make the eyes with half marshmallows and *Smarties*.
7. Make the spectacles with liquorice shoelaces, and use a red *Smartie* for his tongue.
8. Sprinkle muesli around him to represent the soil.
9. Coat a *Marie* biscuit with icing.
10. Decorate the flower with *Smarties* and coloured leaves cut from paper.

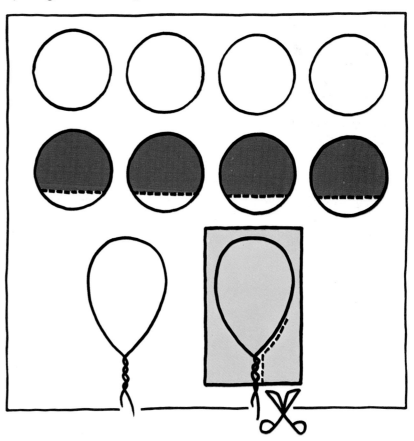

7. Cut off the excess paper and press the wing's wire handles into the bee's body.
8. Colour the desiccated coconut green. Sprinkle around the bee and decorate

Dragon

½ basic cake recipe as on p. 46
4 small jam tins
2½ butter icing recipe as on p. 7
4 different colourings
4 types of sweets, including liquorice
500 mm green florist ribbon
piece of red ribbon
assortment of brightly coloured bits of paper (sweet wrappers)

1. Prepare the cake mixture and bake in four equal parts in round cake tins.
2. Coat each cake with a thin layer of yellow icing. Sandwich the four parts one behind the other, then stand upright. See hint below left.
3. Decorate the bee's body with yellow and brown butter icing using a star-tipped piping tube, alternating the colours. Leave the face end smooth.
4. Pipe the eyes and mouth with brown icing, placing a brown *Smartie* inside each eye.
5. Join two of the wires end to end; then tie their ends to one another, forming a wing shape with a short handle as for *Fairy*, p. 65. Repeat for second wing.
6. Smooth out the yellow serviette or paper on the table, put glue on the wire and place the 'wings' on the paper. Press down firmly and leave to dry.

1. Clean four empty small jam tins and line the inside with waxed paper.
2. Prepare half a cake mixture and bake in the four jam tins.
3. Prepare the icing and divide in four parts. Colour each part differently. Coat each cake with a different colour.
4. Cut one cake in half for the dragon's head. Sandwich the halves together again, but slightly offset, putting the top half more to the back. Cut blocks of liquorice diagonally and insert for teeth. Decorate with an assortment of sweets. Connect the body sections with green ribbons. Use red ribbon for the tongue. Decorate with the bits of paper.

Hint for bee
Cut off a small section at the bottom of each round cake to make it stand more easily (see middle diagram on p. 55).

Hints
1. *Fill the jam tins only halfway with cake mixture to prevent the mixture from spilling over when baking.*
2. *You can use two Swiss Rolls, each cut in half, instead of the cake mixture.*

Beetle

1 basic cake recipe as on p. 46
1 large bowl (160 mm diameter)
1 small bowl (90 mm diameter)
2 butter icing recipe as on p. 7
2 brown *Smarties*
6 round liquorice sweets, pink
2 pink *Jelly Tots*
300 mm lace
200 g desiccated coconut
red colouring
green colouring
silver balls

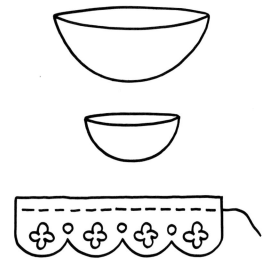

1. Divide cake mixture between bowls and fill each halfway. Bake as described.
2. Coat cakes with bright red butter icing.
3. Make a face on the small cake with two brown *Smarties* for the eyes, pink liquorice sweets for the cheeks and a *Jelly Tot* for the nose. Cut a *Jelly Tot* in half for the mouth.
4. Tack a 300 mm length of lace to fit around the small bowl.
5. Place lace around beetle's head and decorate it further with a star-tipped piping tube.
6. Make a small bow-tie from icing sugar.
7. Cut into round liquorice sweets and remove the black centres; use these for the black spots on the beetle. Do the same for the feet.
8. Colour 200 g desiccated coconut with 2,5 ml green colouring. Mix well to colour all the coconut.
9. Sprinkle coconut around the beetle.

Hints

1. If small chocolate beetles are available, they can be used for further decoration.
2. Small beetles can also be made from instant plastic icing.
3. The two bowls themselves can be used for the beetle's body by placing them upside down and coating them with icing. Decorate further as described. If bowls are filled with confectionery they can be turned over at the party to expose the sweets.

Rag doll

1 basic cake recipe as on p. 46
2 cake tins, 200 mm diameter
1½ metres fine lace
3 butter icing recipe as on p. 7
pink and brown colouring
2 brown *Smarties*
fine paint brush
silver balls
coloured sugar crystals or hundreds and
    thousands
pink satin ribbon

57

1. Divide cake mixture in two and bake in separate tins.
2. Use one cake for the body. Cut a circular section 120 mm in diameter from the centre of the second cake.
3. Cut remaining pieces as shown for the arms and legs.
4. Gather 1½ metres of fine lace for the dress and bonnet.
5. Coat whole body with light pink butter icing.
6. Pipe a ridge of icing around the edge of the body and head to affix the lace.
7. Press down the lace around the edge of the body, starting at one arm and around to the other arm.
8. Do the same for the head from one 'ear' to the other.
9. Pipe sleeves and a bodice for the doll.
10. Pipe five blobs on each hand for the fingers.
11. Use brown icing for shoes and hair.
12. Use silver balls for the buckle and strap.
13. Use two brown *Smarties* for eyes and paint on cheeks, mouth and nose with a fine brush and vegetable colouring.
14. Sprinkle coloured sugar crystals or hundreds and thousands on the remainder of the dress.

Hint
Do not use lace that is too heavy.

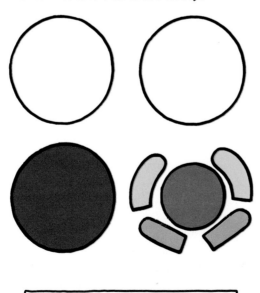

Racing car

1 basic cake recipe as on p. 46
1 cake tin, 250 mm square
2½ butter icing recipe as on p. 7
black colouring
blue colouring
silver balls
gingerbread man
2 lollipops
8 red *Smarties*
8 yellow *Smarties*
1 large lollipop
liquorice blocks

1. Prepare one cake mixture and bake as described.
2. Cut the cake as shown: one broad strip and two narrow ones.
3. Use the broad strip for the car body.
4. Cut one narrow strip in four and form the wheels from these pieces.
5. Use the second narrow strip for the tailfin of the car.
6. Cut a hollow towards the rear of the body for the driver to sit. Cut off a diagonal section across the front of the car to taper it down.

7. Coat the car with blue icing (or let the birthday child decide what colour he would like it to be).

8. Coat each wheel separately with black icing and place in position. Place a *Smartie* of a contrasting colour at the centre of each wheel to form the hub-caps.

9. Use *Smarties*, lollipops or long toffees for the lights and exhausts of the racing car.

10. Make a gingerbread man for the driver, or use a biscuit man.

11. Decorate the car to your own liking with a piping tube, e.g. a number at the front, lines along the sides, etc.

12. Use a lollipop of a suitable colour for the steering wheel.

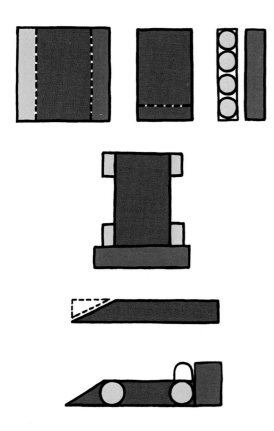

Hint
The chequered flag is made with liquorice all sorts. Peel off the coloured parts with a sharp knife and use only the black and white parts of the sweets.

Tractor

1 basic cake recipe as on p. 46
1 cake tin, 250 mm square
2 butter icing recipe as on p. 7
vegetable colouring of your choice
1 lollipop
1 gingerbread man
liquorice shoelaces and strips
Smarties
All Bran
raisins

1. Prepare one cake mixture and bake in a 250 mm square cake tin.

2. Cut the cake in three equal parts, then divide further as in sketch on p. 60.

3. Use the two halves of the first part for the rear of the tractor. Stack them to make up height.

59

4. Use the second part for the chassis of the tractor.
5. Put the longer section lengthwise for the front with the short section on top of it.
6. The third part is used for the two large wheels at the back and the two smaller wheels at the front.
7. Coat the tractor with coloured icing of your choice, e.g. green, and finish off the edges with liquorice.
8. Seat a gingerbread man on top.
9. Decorate wheels with broad strips of liquorice.
10. Use *Smarties* for headlights and a round lollipop of a suitable colour for the steering wheel.
11. Sprinkle *All Bran* and raisins around the tractor.

Hint
If black colouring is not available, make a darker than usual brown by adding more brown colouring.

Spaceman

1 basic cake recipe as on p. 46
1 round cake tin, 200 mm diameter
1 large jam tin + 2 small jam tins
1 aluminium foil cake plate
2 butter icing recipe as on p. 7
colourful sweets
1 lollipop
2 pipe cleaners, coloured
2 strips aluminium foil, 20 mm x 300 mm
waxed paper

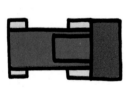
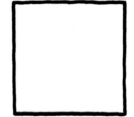

1. Prepare one basic cake recipe as described on p. 46.
2. Clean an empty large jam tin and line on the inside with waxed paper. Half fill with mixture and bake.
3. Bake remainder of the mixture in the round cake tin.
4. Coat large cake with icing and place on the foil plate.
5. Coat smaller cake with icing and place on top of the large one.
6. Decorate the spaceman with various sweets for the eyes, knobs, etc.
7. Wind the pipe cleaners around a pencil to curl them and place on the spaceman's head.
8. Cut two strips of aluminium foil, 20 mm x 300 mm and wind them round a wooden spoon handle. Remove the handle and stick the spiral to the spaceman's body with icing.
9. Clean two empty small jam tins and place under the cake for the spaceman's legs.

Hint
Stick the foil spiral to the body immediately after removing it from the spoon handle as it crinkles and bends easily.

Clown's face

1 basic cake recipe as on p. 46
1 round cake tin, 225 mm diameter
1 round cake tin, 130 mm diameter
2 butter icing recipe as on p. 7, uncoloured
1 butter icing recipe as on p. 7, coloured red
1 packet of *Smarties*
1 small packet of cheese curls or *Nik-Naks*
liquorice shoelaces
2 *Marie* biscuits
1 marshmallow, pink
3 small balloons
hundreds and thousands

1. Use one cake mixture and bake in large and small tins.
2. Cut the small cake as shown and use the parts for the hat.
3. Coat large cake with white icing for the face.

4. Coat the 'hat' with red icing.
5. Make a flower on his hat with one yellow and six green *Smarties*. Stick them on with icing.
6. Use two purple *Smarties* for the eyes and place six pink ones around each eye.
7. Finish off face with liquorice shoelaces.
8. Use a star-tipped piping tube to form the mouth.
9. Coat two Marie biscuits with red icing and decorate with white icing – these make the bowtie.
10. Stick a marshmallow in the middle of the face for the nose and paint it red with red vegetable colouring.
11. Use cheese curls or *Nik-Naks* for the hair.
12. Small balloons can be stuck to his hat with icing.
13. Sprinkle hundreds and thousands around the face.

Hint
A flat floppy knife spreads icing easier than a rigid one.

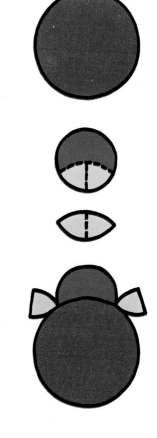

Flower basket

½ basic cake recipe as on p. 46
1 round cake tin, 225 mm diameter
1 butter icing recipe as on p. 7
basket
1 small packet *Jelly Tots*
1 small packet *Smarties*
½ packet marshmallows
hundreds and thousands

1. Prepare and bake half a basic cake recipe.
2. Coat with white butter icing.
3. Place the cake on a doily on a plate.
4. Make flowers as follows: Cut thin slices of marshmallow with a pair of scissors; they form into flower petals automatically. Place the petals around with a *Smartie* at the middle.
5. Smaller flowers can be made using *Jelly Tots* instead of marshmallows.
6. Hundreds and thousands can be strewn over the flowers.
7. Now decorate the top of the cake with the various flowers.
8. Fresh leaves and twigs can be used for further decoration.
9. Place the cake with plate and all inside the basket. Tie a bow on the basket handle.

Hint
Add a doll or rag doll for more decoration. At the same time it can serve as a gift.

Ape

1 basic cake recipe as on p. 46
2 cake tins, approximately 200 mm in diameter
3 butter icing recipe as on p. 7
3 *Marie* biscuits
1 packet chocolate vermicelli
Smarties
1 marshmallow
green and yellow instant plastic icing
thick liquorice for the tail
desiccated coconut, coloured green

1. Prepare the cake mixture, divide between two cake tins and bake.

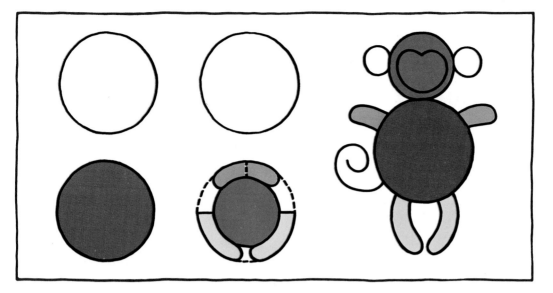

2. Use one cake for the body. Cut a circle 120 mm in diameter from the centre of the second cake for the head.
3. Divide up remaining circular strip for arms and legs (see figure above, below middle).
4. Coat body and head with icing, then the arms and legs.
5. Coat the *Marie* biscuits with icing, then press two of them into chocolate vermicelli for ears.
6. Cut two grooves on the top side of the head to fit the ape's ears. Prop them up with icing at the base of each ear.
7. Cut third biscuit for the mouth and nose. Outline the mouth with a liquorice shoelace.
8. Use half a marshmallow and a brown *Smartie* for each eye.
9. Sprinkle chocolate vermicelli on his body and use a length of thick liquorice for the tail.
10. Form green leaves and yellow bananas with instant plastic icing.
11. Sprinkle green desiccated coconut around the ape.

Hint
When sprinkling vermicelli on the body, hold the index finger against the side to press down the bits that fall over the side.

Owl

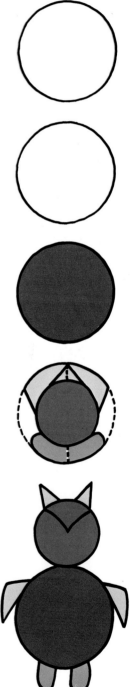

1 basic cake mixture as on p. 46
2 round cake tins, 200 mm diameter
3 butter icing recipe as on p. 7
orange and brown colouring
8 small chocolate *Flakes*
6 jelly beans
2 white marshmallows
2 brown *Smarties*
10 round white sweets
desiccated coconut, coloured green

1. Prepare the basic cake mixture and bake in two 200 mm round cake tins.
2. Use one cake for the owl's body.
3. Cut up the other cake in sections for the two feet, two wings and two ears, as shown in the sketch.
4. Colour the icing with half a teaspoon of both brown and orange vegetable colouring.
5. Coat the whole cake with orange-brown icing.
6. Break four *Flakes* in small pieces and sprinkle over the owl's body where shown on the photograph on p. 62.
7. Use two white marshmallows and two brown *Smarties* for the eyes and a jelly bean for the beak.
8. Sprinkle green desiccated coconut around the owl. Use the other four *Flakes* to make tree branches.
9. Make more owl faces as in step 7, one for each year of the child's age, and put a candle on each.

Bear's face

½ basic mixture as on p. 46
1 round cake tin, 225 mm diameter
½ cooked frosting recipe as on p. 8
brown colouring
3 *Marie* biscuits
liquorice shoelace
2 brown *Smarties*
gift wrapping with a bear motif

Hint
The cooked frosting should be used immediately after preparation, as it hardens quickly.

1. Prepare mixture and bake in a round cake tin.
2. Place cake on a prepared base.
3. Prepare half a recipe of cooked frosting and add brown vegetable colouring.
4. Coat the cake with frosting.
5. Coat *Marie* biscuits with frosting as well and place in position on the cake for ears and mouth.
6. Use liquorice shoelace for the nose.
7. Use two *Smarties* for the eyes.
8. Gift wrapping with a bear motif can be used for background.

Bicycle

1 basic cake mixture as on p. 46
2 round cake tins, 200 mm diameter
17 Boudoir finger biscuits
2 butter icing recipe as on p. 7
2 *Smarties*
1 packet silver balls
1 packet liquorice strips
hundreds and thousands
red and black or brown colouring

1. Bake basic cake mixture in two round cake tins.
2. Place the cakes on a foil-covered base more than the length of a finger biscuit apart.
3. Stick together six pairs of finger biscuits and coat with red icing.
4. Place one pair at an angle between the wheels (see photograph).
5. Place two pairs horizontally between the tops of the wheels.
6. Place one pair vertically above the front wheel and use two pairs for the handle bars.
7. The thirteenth finger biscuit is cut in half, then sandwiched together and coated with icing as the others. Place vertically for the saddle support.
8. The saddle can be made with a piece of cake, or four finger biscuits can be sandwiched together in two pairs, which are then coated with black or brown icing.
9. Coat wheels with red icing. Place a *Smartie* at each wheel centre. Use several rows of silver balls for spokes.
10. Surround each wheel with strips of liquorice for tyres.

11. Coat base foil around the bicycle with a thin layer of icing and sprinkle with hundreds and thousands.
12. A black, blue or yellow bicycle can be made in the same way.

Fairy

1 basic cake mixture as on p. 46
cake plate
2 butter icing recipe as on p. 7
1 plastic doll
cling wrap
4 x 270 mm lengths florist wire
1 yellow serviette or paper
glue
small flowers
aluminium foil strip

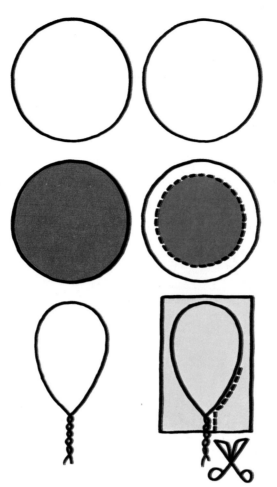

The drawing below indicates how the wings of the fairy are made.

Hint
The 'dress' can also be decorated entirely with small coloured meringues

1. Prepare and bake the basic cake mixture in two cake tins.
2. Place one cake on a cake plate and coat top with icing.
3. Place the second layer on top and trim the edge at an angle from the top outwards to the bottom layer.
4. Make a small hole in the centre to place the doll.
5. Remove the doll's legs and wrap the body, not face, in cling wrap. Keep the legs separate to present later.
6. Place the doll in the hole to just below the arms.
7. Coat the whole 'dress' (cake) with icing.
8. Use a star-tipped piping tube to decorate the 'dress' from the top downwards.
9. Join two of the wires end to end; then tie their ends to one another, forming a wing shape with a short handle. Repeat for the second wing.
10. Smooth out the yellow serviette or paper on the table, put glue on the wire and place the 'wing' on the paper. Press down firmly and leave to dry.
11. Trim off the excess paper and press the handle of the wings into the cake at the fairy's back.
12. Place little flowers in her hair and randomly on her dress.
13. Make a wand with a strip of foil.

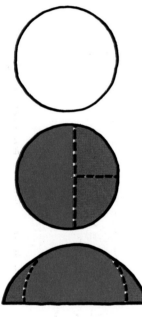

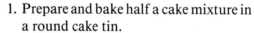

Umbrella

½ basic cake mixture as on p. 46
1 round cake tin, 225 mm diameter
2 butter icing recipe as on p. 7
1 candy stick
340 mm lace
small sweets and flowers
hundreds and thousands

1. Prepare and bake half a cake mixture in a round cake tin.
2. Cut off a strip at the bottom of the cake as shown in the sketch (see red section), and halve that section again.
3. Use the latter two pieces to form the bottom corners of the umbrella.
4. Coat the entire cake with pink icing.
5. Use a thick candy stick for the handle.
6. Use a straight strip of lace to finish off the umbrella.
7. Decorate the umbrella with small sweets and sprinkle with hundreds and thousands.
8. Tie a bow around the candy stick and decorate with flowers.

Hint
Break off about 50 mm of the long end of the candy stick and place at the top of the umbrella. This prevents the cake from see-sawing on the candy stick, and makes for a longer looking handle.

Ice-cream cone cake

½ basic cake mixture as on p. 46
1 round cake tin, 225 mm diameter
½ cooked frosting recipe, as on p. 8
1 round red lollipop
7 (ice-cream) cones

1. Prepare and bake half a cake mixture in a round tin.
2. Cut off a section at the bottom as shown in the figure below.
3. Prepare cooked frosting and coat the cake.
4. Cut the ice-cream cones in half lengthwise with a sharp serrated knife.
5. Arrange the cone halves against the cut-off bottom of the cake downwards as though to form a large cone.
6. Top off the 'ice-cream' with a red lollipop.

Hint
When cutting the cones, start at the open end and cut only the one side, then the other side.

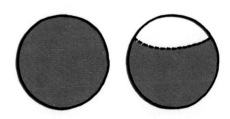

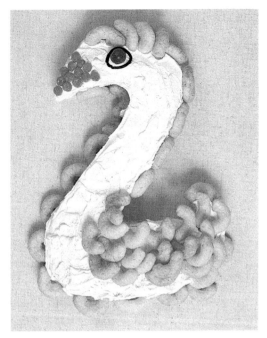

Number cakes

One

1 basic cake recipe as on p. 46
1 bread baking tin, 105 mm x 280 mm
1 bread baking tin, 100 mm x 190 mm
2 packets of *Smarties*
2 butter icing recipe as on p. 7
blue and red vegetable colouring

1. Divide cake mix between two baking tins.
2. Use shortest of the two cakes for the bottom part of the 'candle'.
3. Cut off a piece of the longer cake for the candle flame as indicated on the sketch in the second column.
4. Place the longer section above the shorter base.
5. Coat the candle with blue icing and a little white icing or frosting at the top.
6. Coat the flame with red icing.
7. Decorate with *Smarties* at the lower end of the candle.

Two

1 basic cake recipe as on p. 46
1 cake tin, 250 mm square
icing
½ frosting as on p. 8
yellow vegetable colouring
1 packet *Smarties*
½ packet *Flings*

1. Bake cake mix in a cake tin 250 mm square.
2. Cut the required sections from the cake as shown on the sketch on the right.
3. Put the sections together with icing.
4. Prepare frosting, add a little yellow colouring and coat the cake.
5. Make duck's beak and eye with orange *Smarties*.
6. Arrange *Flings* for the duck's feathers, especially on the wings.

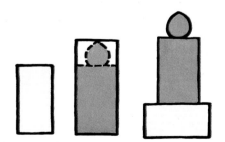

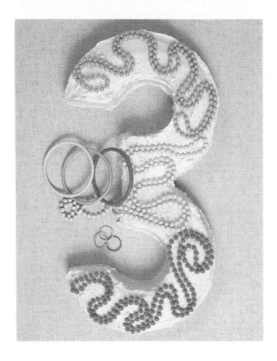

Three

1 basic cake recipe as on p. 46
2 round cake tins, 200 mm diameter
2 butter icing recipe as on p. 7
3 plastic bangles
3 plastic rings
3 strings plastic beads

1. Use cake recipe and divide the mix between the two tins.
2. Cut out the sections as shown in sketch.
3. Place the two half-circles below one another to form a figure 3.
4. Coat cake on all sides with white icing.
5. Use plastic rings, beads and bangles to decorate the cake in patterns of your choice.

Four

1 basic cake recipe as on p. 46
1 rectangular cake tin of about 105 mm x 280 mm
1 rectangular cake tin of about 110 mm x 330 mm
2 butter icing recipe as on p. 7
4 coloured plastic pairs of scissors for decoration

1. Divide cake mix between two tins and bake.
2. Place the longer cake vertically. Cut off pieces of the other to form the rest of the figure 4, as shown below.
3. Coat cake with coloured icing of your choice.
4. Use four plastic pairs of scissors to decorate cake.

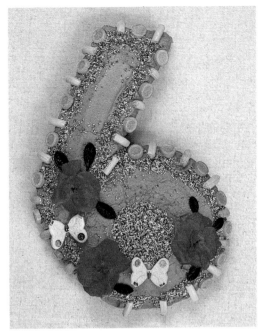

Five

1½ basic cake recipe as on p. 46
2 cake tins, 100 mm x 190 mm
1 round cake tin, 200 mm diameter
2 butter icing recipe as on p. 7
48 meringues of three different colours

1. Prepare basic cake recipe, divide mix between cake tins and bake.
2. Use one small cake for the top bar of the 5, and the other for the vertical bar.
3. Cut circular part from the large cake, as shown. Coat whole cake with white icing and decorate with the meringues.

Six

1 basic cake recipe as on p. 46
1 cake tin, 105 mm x 280 mm
1 round cake tin, 200 mm diameter
2 butter icing recipe as on p. 7
2,5 ml pink vegetable colouring
fresh pink flowers
long pink toffees
round pink sweets
hundreds and thousands

1. Prepare cake recipe and divide mix between the baking tins and bake.
2. Form a figure 6 as shown in the sketch below. Do not cut out the centre part of the round cake.
3. Add half a teaspoon of vegetable colouring to icing, mix well and coat cake.
4. Decorate with long pink toffees and round pink sweets. Place fresh flowers on the cake and sprinkle with hundreds and thousands.

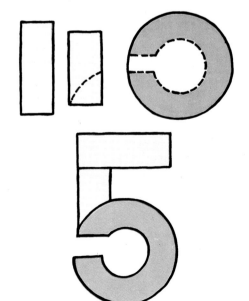

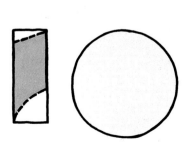

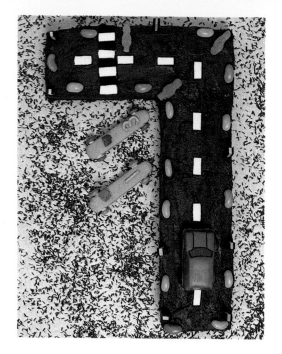

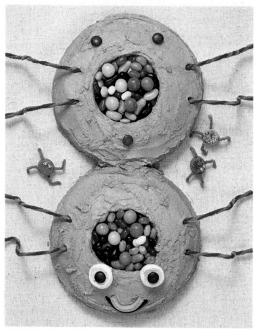

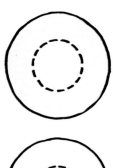

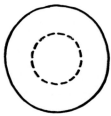

Seven

1 basic cake recipe as on p. 46
1 cake tin, 105 mm x 280 mm
1 cake tin, 110 mm x 330 mm
2 butter icing recipe as on p. 7
1 teaspoon chocolate colouring
liquorice allsorts and jelly beans

1. Prepare basic recipe and divide between baking tins and bake.
2. Place the shorter cake at the top of the figure 7, and use the longer cake for the upright.
3. Mix one teaspoon of chocolate colouring with icing and coat cake.
4. Place liquorice strips along the 'road'.
5. Remove coloured parts of the liquorice allsorts and cut the white squares to make white lines for the road and pedestrian crossing.
6. A racing car and robot can be added.
7. Decorate with jelly beans (see photograph).

Eight

1 basic cake recipe as on p. 46
2 round cake tins, 200 m diameter
2 butter icing recipe as on p. 7
brown colouring
2 brown *Smarties*
1 marshmallow and 1 toffee
8 green pipe cleaners
8 red pipe cleaners
2 packets mixed sweets

1. Prepare basic cake recipe, divide between the cake tins and bake.
2. Cut out a circular section from the centre of each cake (see figure below left).
3. Coat cake with light brown icing.
4. Cut a marshmallow in two and add a brown *Smartie* for each eye. A toffee can be bent for the mouth.
5. Twist pairs of pipe cleaners of different colours together and bend in the form of legs. Make eight legs and place in position as shown on photograph.
6. Fill the centres of the cakes with an assortment of sweets.

Nine

1 basic cake recipe as on p. 46
1 round cake tin of approximately 200 mm in diameter
1 rectangular cake tin, 110 mm x 330 mm
2 butter icing recipe as on p. 7
round liquorice sweets with white centres
1 packet liquorice shoelaces

1. Prepare and divide the cake mix between the tins and bake.
2. Coat both cakes with white icing.
3. Arrange the cakes to form a figure 9.
4. Use round white liquorice sweets cut in half to make the musical notes.
5. Use liquorice shoelaces to complete the notes' tails.

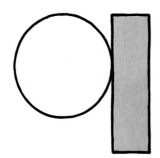

Ten

1 basic chocolate cake recipe as on p. 46
1 rectangular cake tin, approximately 100 mm x 190 mm
1 round cake tin, approximately 200 mm in diameter
1 butter icing recipe as on p. 7
3 small packets of nut chocolate
2 *Flakes*
3 chocolate biscuits

1. Divide the basic cake mix between the baking tins and bake.
2. Coat both cakes with butter icing.
3. Decorate the sides with nut chocolate.
4. Make a large clock using *Flakes* for the hands.
5. Pipe the numbers 1 to 12 with a star-tipped piping tube.
6. Put chocolate biscuits as small clocks on the oblong cake.
7. Again, pipe on numbers and hands on the smaller clocks.

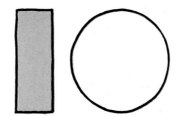

Adventure cakes

This type of cake is very popular, especially with the smaller children. It consists basically of a cardboard box framework which is decorated with interesting food. The idea is to make all the food at the party part of the construction so that it is fun to eat and fun to discover.

General hints

1. The size of box to be used depends on the design. Just about any type of box can be utilised from wine cartons, oats boxes and shoe boxes to bottle cartons, plastic bottles, wine bottle cylinders and all sorts of small boxes.
2. First cover the boxes with aluminium foil.
3. Join various parts of the box construction to one another using masking tape or staples.
4. The number of cakes, sweets and biscuits depends on the size of the 'cake'.
5. Sweets and biscuits are stuck to the aluminium foil with royal icing.
6. Use a firm base, for example a tray or plank.

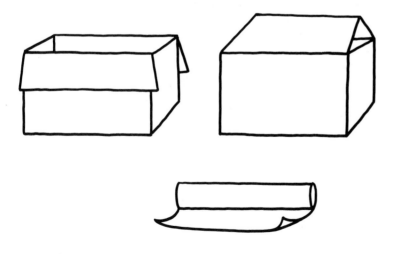

The clown above is a
diagram of the photograph
appearing on p. 6.

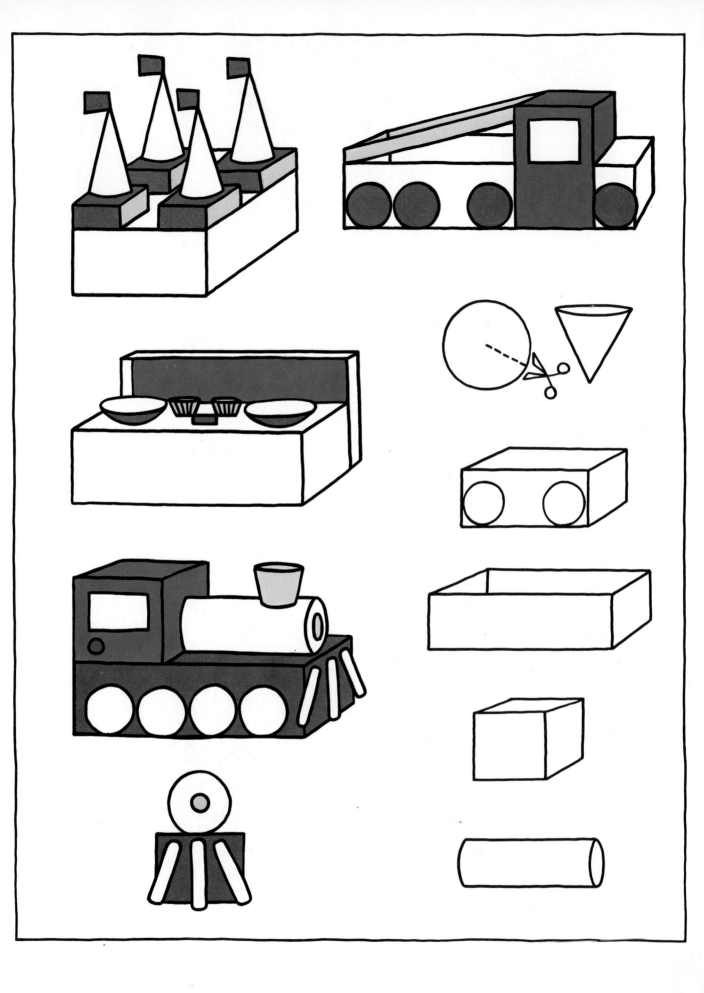

The castle above left is made of an open cardboard box which is cut around the upper edge to form machicolations. Place wine cartons at the corners and cut an opening in the front wall to form a drawbridge. The photographs on this page illustrate the different steps in the construction of a fort.

Opposite page, from bottom left to top right: the front view of a locomotive, the locomotive itself, a scale, castle and tip-truck. The line drawings below the truck go with the locomotive and are, from top to bottom: a cone for the funnel, a cardboard box or ice-cream container which could serve as goods carriage, a shoe-box (turn it upside down for the undercarriage), an oatmeal box for the engine-house and a wine carton for the boiler (cut a hole in front for the funnel). The drawings are all self-explanatory and on the basis of them one should be able to construct the 'cakes' with relative ease. Decorate them as preferred, using icing, sweets, biscuits and confectionery (see notes on p. 72 and compare the photograph below right and the one on p. 6).

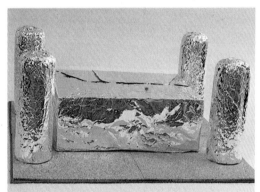

Activities and games

Activities

Drawing album

The pre-school child cannot always express his feelings in words but here he will have the chance to draw something for his friend on his birthday.

paper
crayons

1. Give each child at the party a sheet of paper and crayons, and ask them to draw a picture.
2. Write their names on the completed drawings.
3. Staple them together in book form. Now the birthday boy or girl has a memento from each of his or her friends.

Masks

paper plates
wool
paint
elastic

1. Give each child a paper plate.
2. Allow the children to decorate the plates with pieces of wool and to colour in the nose and rings around the eyes with paint.
3. Pierce a hole on both sides of the mask and tie elastic through it. Now they can enjoy the masquerade!

Bread faces

500 ml buttermilk
1 cube yeast
1 ml bicarbonate of soda
10 ml salt
25 ml sugar
30 ml margarine
480 to 600 g (4 or 5 x 250 ml) cake flour

1. Slowly heat the buttermilk to lukewarm. Mix it with the yeast, bicarbonate of soda, salt, sugar and margarine.
2. Gradually work in the cake flour with the above mixture. Knead for about 5 minutes.
3. Set the oven to 40°C. Place a lid on top of the bowl with dough and leave to rise in the oven.
4. Allow the dough to rise to double its volume and knead.
5. Set the oven to 180°C.
6. Give each child a small ball of dough and let them mould animals or faces, etc. Place the mouldings on a greased baking sheet and bake for 10 to 15 minutes, until light brown.

Decorated butter-biscuits

240 g (250 ml) margarine
100 g (125 ml) sugar
vanilla essence
360 g (750 ml) cake flour
sweets, hundreds and thousands, liquorice, cherries, etc.

1. Beat together the margarine, sugar and vanilla and work this into the flour.
2. Roll out this mixture to approximately 12 mm thick on a surface lightly sprinkled with flour.
3. Provide bowls with sweets, hundreds and thousands, cherries, liquorice, etc. and allow the children to decorate the butter-biscuits themselves.
4. Bake at 180°C for 10 to 15 minutes.

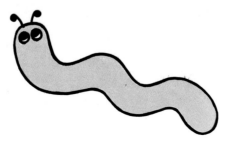

Bread flowers

white or brown bread
margarine
cucumber, parsley and watercress
cheese, tomatoes and eggs
cottage cheese
decorations

1. Slice bread in thin slices.
2. Let children press out shapes with a biscuit cutter or drinking glass.
3. Spread with cottage cheese or margarine.
4. Put bread on a plate and place on the table with bowls of cucumber strips, parsley, watercress, cheese cubes, tomato and hard-boiled eggs.
5. The children can now decorate their bread flowers to their hearts' content.

Games

Blind man's buff

Blindfold one playmate who stands in the middle of a room. The other children run around him while he tries to touch one of them. When someone is touched, he must stand still and make any kind of noise. If the blind man guesses who it is, the 'discovered' child takes a turn at being blindfolded.

Falcon and hen

The mother of the birthday child plays the hen and protects all her chickens against the falcon. The falcon is one of the playmates and the rest of the group are chickens. The hen spreads her arms like wings for protection while the falcon tries to grab one of her chickens. It continues until all the chickens have been caught.

Pass the bag

Everybody sits around a circle drawn on the ground or grass, or a hosepipe can be used to make a circle. One child stands in the centre and plays a musical instrument while the others in the circle pass a bean bag or handkerchief to one another. The moment the music stops, the one holding the bag wins a turn to play the instrument.

Fishing

Take a dowel stick and tie a magnet with a piece of string to the end as a fishing rod. Cut out a paper fish for each of the playmates and write a number on each fish. Put a paper clip on each one for the magnet to cling to. Each guest gets a chance to catch a fish. The number on the fish he catches corresponds to a small gift or sweet in the fish pond.

Balloons

Bring all the children together and tell them that they are all balloons, except for one who is the 'pin'. When the 'pin' shouts: 'Let the balloons go!' all the 'balloons' must run away because if the 'pin' touches them they will burst and be out of the game. The 'balloon' lasting the longest is the winner.

Follow the string

Take a very long string and tie one end to any object, e.g. a tree. Then unwind the string all through the house and garden, tying a small gift to the other end. It can be a bag of sweets for the winner to distribute between the others. The game can be repeated.

Who can blow the biggest bubble?

Ball game

Divide the children into two teams. Take a large washing basket and three large balls to throw into the basket. Each team stands about two metres from the basket and in turn tries to throw as many balls as possible into the basket. One team member stands behind the basket to return the balls and to keep score of the number of balls thrown in. The team with the highest score in a given time wins.

Blow soccer

Half the children stand on opposite sides of a large table and a table tennis ball is placed in the middle of the table. Everybody starts blowing, trying to blow off the ball at the opponents' end of the table. A point is scored with every ball blown off the opponents' end.

Crabs and Crows

Divide the children into two equal teams, Crabs and Crows. Two lines, about ten metres apart, are drawn and the teams take up positions. About ten metres behind each line a further line is drawn. Someone stands in the centre and shouts either 'Crabs!' or 'Crows!'.

If he shouts 'Crabs'!, the Crabs must run to catch the Crows before they reach the second line behind them. Those caught before the safety line join the other team, and so on.

Blowing bubbles

Add liquid soap to a jug full of water. Mix well and give each child a smaller jug half full of soapy water and a drinking straw. Now they can have a bubble-blowing competition. The one to blow the most or biggest bubbles is the winner.

Deer hunt

Draw a large circle and a number of children (deer) stand inside it. Two hunters stand on opposite sides of the circle, some distance away. They try to hit the 'deer' inside the circle with a ball. Those hit must leave the circle. The last 'deer' to survive is the winner.

Frog race

Cut a few frogs from thin white paper and place them next to one another on the carpet or floor. A line is drawn on the other side of the room as the finishing line. A child kneels behind each frog and all start simultaneously to blow the frogs forward. The first frog across the finishing line is the winner. The children are not allowed to turn or move the frogs by hand.

Riddles

All sit around the table with their hands in their laps. One child has a bag with an assortment of small articles. He alone knows what they are. One article is taken out of the bag and given from hand to hand under the table.

Each one must silently guess what the article is, but must not tell until the article has done the round. The first one to guess correctly, receives it as a reward and takes a turn handing out the articles.

Catch the bag

Use a bean bag. One child starts, throws the bag in the air and shouts someone's name. If the child who is called catches the bag on the first try, he gets a reward. Give everyone a chance to try and catch the bag.